DRAMA and the ADOLESCENT JOURNEY

Warm-ups and Activities to Address Teen Issues

Linda Ruth Hodges Nelson
and
Lanell René Kemp Finneran

Foreword by Patricia Sternberg

HEINEMANN
Portsmouth, NH

Heinemann
A division of Reed Elsevier Inc.
361 Hanover Street
Portsmouth, NH 03801–3912
www.heinemanndrama.com

Offices and agents throughout the world

© 2006 by Linda Nelson and Lanell Finneran.

Library of Congress Cataloging-in-Publication Data
Nelson, Linda.
    Drama and the adolescent journey : warm-ups and activities to address teen issues / Linda Nelson and Lanell Finneran.
        p. cm.
    Includes bibliographical references.
    ISBN 0-325-00851-5 (alk. paper)
    1. Teenagers—Counseling of. 2. Adolescent psychotherapy. 3. Drama—Therapeutic use. 4. Adolescence. I. Finneran, Lanell. II. Title.
    HV1421.N45 2006
    616.89'15230835—dc22   2005035984

Editor: Lisa A. Barnett
Production management: Renée Le Verrier
Production coordination: Patricia Adams
Composition: Tom Allen/Pear Graphic Design
Cover design: Jenny Jenson Greenleaf
Manufacturing: Steve Bernier

Printed in the United States of America on acid-free paper.
10 09 08 07 06   VP   1 2 3 4 5

CONTENTS

ACKNOWLEDGMENTS

The authors owe a debt of gratitude to Sally Bailey, who spawned this idea, and to the students at Kansas State University and the University of Wyoming, who served as the catalysts for this project and provided much practical information for this text. They also wish to thank Patricia Sternberg, professor at Hunter College, for her faith in this project and her willingness to mentor them in the publishing process. And a special thanks goes to Lisa Barnett, our editor, who saw the potential for this manuscript and worked with us to see it to its completion.

The authors know that no educational processes are complete without the students, and they owe much gratitude to the public school students in both Casper, Wyoming, and in Lawrence, Kansas, who participated in the many activities included in this book. Some of their photos are included here, as well. Of course, no work is done entirely by its authors. We give special thanks to our husbands, Ralph Nelson and Robert Finneran, for their willingness to support us and give us those necessary hours of solitude to complete this project.

FOREWORD

Adolescence is often described as a kind of No Man's Land existing somewhere between childhood and the legal age of twenty-one. Known in our modern world as a tumultuous time when young people push the boundaries as far as they can go, it is a time when one minute they are desperate for adulthood and all the privileges therein, and the next minute they want to crawl back to the safety of home and parental approval. Yet, these are the years in which many major decisions for life's directions are made. Oftentimes, these decisions are designed with no thought to consequences. Where and how are young people to gain the experience for well-informed choices? If they are lucky, they have a support system of caring parents, knowledgeable teachers, and other interested adults in their lives with whom they can communicate. However, few adolescents sail through these years with little or no emotional difficulties. The lucky ones have an outlet for their exploration of emotions through sports, arts, music, or theatre. These areas necessitate a certain amount of talent or natural ability. What of the others?

Drama can be the outlet for adolescents regardless of their talents or abilities. Those of us who have spent our lives in the field know that drama is the answer because everyone can do drama no matter what their functional level. There is a clear distinction between drama and theatre, which this book emphasizes. Simply put, *Drama is the* **process***, while theatre is the* **product***.* This book discusses *drama* and shows how the *process* presents a way for adolescents to try out new behaviors and new roles within the safe confines of drama games, exercises, and various creative arts activities.

The authors ask the reader to remember his or her own adolescence. When most of us look back, we wonder how we made it through certain crises, those turning points in which we could have gone in one direction or another. Those of us who were lucky enough to have the arts, and especially drama, remember what a great outlet for emotions it was and is. When we played a role different from ourselves, we lost our particular inadequacies for the moment and put ourselves in that person's shoes. Even if we were shy, we could play an assertive queen in a fairy tale or take on the role of a clown in an improvisation. Most of us discovered what fun it was to play a role different from ourselves.

The importance of working with youth cannot be emphasized enough. Young people are vulnerable and fragile during those adolescent years, while at the same time in a great hurry to grow up. The desire to seem grown up often overshadows the reality of their limited knowledge and understanding. The more opportunities adolescents have to try out new behaviors, try on new roles, and expand their own role repertoire, the more ability they gain in understanding who they are and who they want to be.

Linda Nelson and Lanell Finneran have more than fifty years combined experience between them, working with a variety of different youth groups at different age and functional levels. They bring a combination of teacher, therapist, and drama specialist to their work, as well as solid theoretical knowledge based on academic research plus clinical experience. The authors urge their readers to understand the "why" of their activities before they begin the "how to." They acknowledge the stages of moral development and remind us that decisions made at these crossroads have long-term effects.

While there are numerous books on Creative Drama, Interactive Drama, and Theatre in Education, as well as Drama Therapy texts, none of these focus primarily on the adolescent. *Drama and the Adolescent Journey* does just that. It is a much-needed guide that offers a map for navigating the turbulent waters of adolescence with the swift currents and undertows that push and pull in ever-changing directions. While role-playing is often the primary focus in many drama groups, this book offers drama activities that not only include role-play but also go far beyond that simple format to involve meaningful growth activities. It underscores the value of moving between fantasy and reality by telling stories, improvising scenes, or creating monologues—while at all times keeping the material fictional.

The authors point out that the primary concern of adolescence is discovering one's own identity. "What do I want to be when I grow up? Who do I want to be?" Drama offers the ideal tool for discovering one's identity. Since adolescents spend a great deal of their time and energy in the process of socialization, drama offers an active way to explore questions of identity and examine difficult decisions. It gives young people a way to investigate problems in a non-threatening, safe environment, using metaphor to maintain distance from the personal self.

This book moves smoothly from solid academic theory to practical suggestions with a variety of drama activities. It identifies some old favorites but explains enough new and innovative ideas to interest both the seasoned professional as well as the new-comer. It specifies many of the usual problems that arise with adolescent groups and emphasizes the importance of structure, with a format to follow. It also provides the necessary background for persons in the helping professions who desire to enliven the group process.

Like sports and academics, drama demands concentration. It promotes and values the importance of the imagination, where all the arts begin, and teaches us how to expand role repertoire. Only after an extended period of experimenting with different roles do adolescents become capable of deciding which role fits them best. Coming back full circle to the question, "Who do you want to be?"

The joy the authors share in their work comes through in all the information and advice they give us. Their energy and enthusiasm shines through all their examples. They understand the problems and pitfalls of adolescence and value and respect the young people with whom they work. They meet the different challenges of those who are beginning their adolescent journey to those who have almost reached the goal of adulthood. Along with the games, exercises, and activities in the book, the authors give this advice to those who would follow their lead in drama: Share the journey in a manner that is both productive and delightful for each of you.

—Patricia Sternberg, RDT/BCT

INTRODUCTION

In the fall of 1999, Linda Nelson was approached about teaching a summer course, Drama Therapy with Adolescents, for the University of Wyoming. Foolishly enthusiastic and willing to tackle a new challenge, she agreed to do so. Although she had never seen a text for such a course, she set about searching for one that would adequately address developmental tasks of adolescence, the theoretical basis for drama therapy, and a variety of tried and tested drama therapy approaches with adolescents. In that process, she discovered several books that addressed effective exercises to use with teen drama groups, including several that approached the issue of improvisational theatre with teens. She was once again introduced to works of such persons as Piaget and Erickson, who so eloquently outlined the developmental tasks of adolescence. She discovered almost no books that addressed drama therapy with adolescents and children, and those that did so were written for a very narrow audience of drama therapists who already have a firm basis in the theoretical work in this field.

Linda managed to teach the summer course, putting together a variety of professional articles and a couple of books on improvisational theatre, and supplementing those written materials with information regarding her own personal experiences in working with adolescents. That same summer, Lanell Finneran was teaching a Creative Art Therapies course for Kansas State University, putting together her own text for that course as well. At the end of the summer, Sally Bailey, director of the drama therapy program at Kansas State University, approached both Linda and Lanell, suggesting that they write a book on the subject of drama therapy with adolescents. Thoroughly schooled in spontaneity by their work with drama therapy and foolish because of their work with adolescents, they agreed to tackle this project.

This book provides the necessary background for persons in the helping professions (mental health practitioners, educators, and youth workers) who desire to enliven the group process. Experienced professionals hopefully will discover new techniques they can use in their practice. Persons new to the field can profit from the theoretical bases laid in the book and gradually begin to incorporate drama into their work. The journey of adolescence is enlivened with energy and open to possibilities. May readers find both energy and possibility, to combine with their own creativity, in the following chapters.

1

THE ADOLESCENT JOURNEY

You see them everywhere—embarking on the journey, getting stalled at the crossroad, taking a questionable footpath through the dense, dark forest, and eventually arriving at a destination. Some leave in the middle of winter with only a tank top, shorts, and sandals. Some slip on boulders in their pathway and emerge with scars that last a lifetime. Some move cautiously along the well-worn path, fearful of their own shadows. Some stand out more than others do.

Adults sometimes have forgotten about the journey. Peter Blos calls this forgetfulness the "amnestic veil" (Blos 1962, 116). The veil allows adults to remember the experience but forget most of the emotions. It allows the adult to remember the crew cut, the first drink, the first menstrual cycle, and the loss of virginity. But the fear, self-consciousness, anxiety, and wonder associated with those teenage experiences become less accessible to the adult memory.

As we embark on this adolescent journey together, take the risk of remembering your own journey. The journey that seemed so very exciting when you were a young child, the journey that was full of wonder, adventure, and even a little peril. Try to remember the preparations you made for that journey. What did you put in your own backpack? How did you dress for the journey? What did you do when you lost the map and compass? Did someone else accompany you on this journey? What was the weather like? Did you pick up any souvenirs along the way? And most importantly, what are the most long-lasting impressions that you have of this trip?

The journey taken in adolescence goes in all directions, as any adult will attest. As youth move from childhood to adulthood, they develop intellectually, emotionally, physically, and spiritually. While these developmental phases may occur at different times and rates, each individual youth experience incorporates all of these aspects. As we examine the journey of adolescence, we shall examine these four developmental aspects as milestones in the journey.

FOLLOWING THE MAP: INTELLECTUAL DEVELOPMENT

Let's begin this adolescent journey with a map. Some adolescents, of course, choose to forego map reading, just as they fail to heed warnings along the way. But a journey must begin somewhere. For the sake of examining intellectual development, we shall begin our journey in the east, the place of birth, where morning dawns. From birth, the child has begun this process of intellectual development. The recognition of familiar faces, the exploration of body parts, and the gradual acquisition of language consume most of the first year of life. The adolescent continues this process of intellectual development in fits and starts. The early adolescent is so consumed by emotional development that intellectual pursuits are put on hold for several years. Just witness the middle school or junior high teacher trying to engage students in academic endeavors. While the brain is certainly capable of intellectual pursuits at this age, early teens are often so distracted by peers, acne, and rapid physical growth that they take little time to engage in intellectual endeavors. While adults recognize that young adolescents are certainly in need of a map for their journey, young teens are much more concerned about whether it looks "cool" to be seen consulting anything. If teens become stuck at this point in their development, they may never achieve their goals. Frequently grades slip, and the culture of peers becomes so all-consuming that teens never rebound sufficiently to recapture the sense of their own future.

By the time teens have reached high school, the middle adolescent years, they are usually much more clearly focused on intellectual pursuits. They may enjoy intellectual sparring with adults in an effort to see if they can intellectually overpower the adults. When intellectual efforts are rewarded with good grades, as well as with plaques and trophies for academic achievements, students gain both pride and a sense of independence.

Choices About the Future

Although teens may remain rather unfocused in their career choices, the future takes on more significance. The question of "What do I want to do when I grow up?" increases in urgency as teens prepare to leave home and enter college, the military, or the world of work. Schneider and Stevenson in *The Ambitious Generation* (1999) argue that far too many teenagers simply focus on getting into college, rather than obtaining the proper preparation for entering a career. Although highly motivated, they lack direction. This argument seems to say that adolescents focus on the next immediate step beyond high school but sometimes are unable to focus on long-range goals. They seem unaware of educational requirements for specific career interests and unaware of the needs of the labor market. They may choose highly competitive fields with relatively few job openings rather than examining the exigencies of the labor market to determine where jobs may be obtained in the near future. Because they lack a coherent plan, they are often easily derailed. Although they may have some idea where the road is going, once they get distracted, they find it difficult to find an alternate route to their destination.

Abstract and Moral Reasoning

At this stage of their development, they have entered the formal operations stage. They are capable of dealing with hypothetical situations and more complex deductive reasoning. Because of these newly developed skills, they enjoy imagining what is possible as well as what is real (Piaget 1981). They are capable of more abstract reasoning and wish to draw their own conclusions. They are also quite idealistic and can become easily absorbed in activities that allow them to create their own utopian communities. Their lack of experience does not thwart their ability to create logical arguments. Although they are more willing to consult the map for this journey, they may disagree with the map if it does not fit their own perception of the world.

While lacking in experience, teenagers are still capable of

suggesting alternatives. Ask the parents of a teen how often they have become embroiled in heated arguments because they are trying to uphold the standards and values of the family or community. Teens, fully capable of abstract reasoning, can argue for hours about how things should be, rather than how things are. So even if we offer adolescents a map for their journey, they may disagree with the directives.

Adolescents often engage in moral reasoning. Those who are more capable of higher abstract reasoning may also be capable of an elevated moral reasoning ability. But the two capabilities do not necessarily develop concurrently. Lawrence Kohlberg (1984) defines six stages of moral development. However, since he saw so few individuals at stage six, that aspect of the principled conscience will not be examined. In stage one, elementary school children normally adhere to the principles of right and wrong that have been presented to them by an authority figure. They see that they are to obey, and if they do not do so, they will be punished. As children move into stage two, they begin to act in their own best interest, seeing an exchange of good for good and bad for bad. Kohlberg finds most teens at level three or four, with occasional responses above or below these stages. In stage three, they do what is socially acceptable to others. If they move into stage four, they may make moral judgments based on a respect for authority and the desire to maintain the social order. Youth see themselves as members of the community, with responsibilities to that community. However, they see social relations simply as extensions of interpersonal relationships. Rarely would teens move into stage five, which involves a genuine concern for the welfare of others, based on an understanding of the social contract of all humanity.

Carol Gilligan (1982) suggests that males and females base their moral judgments on different premises. She notes that most developmental theory is based on a male model, where moral judgments are primarily determined on the basis of justice. Females, on the other hand, base their judgments on relationships and center moral issues around questions of care. As adolescents begin to struggle with issues of autonomy, these differences become more predominant. Males may see their independence as offering freedom from personal relationships, while females see independence as the establishment of different personal relationships. Take a typical high school election campaign as an example. Males will run for office, declaring what they hope to do for the student body. They may suggest more rights for students or better privileges in the school forum. Females, while they may tout some of the same issues, will largely base their campaign around relationship issues such as trust, reliability, and honesty.

Adolescents can easily become engaged in altruistic concerns such as a Habitat for Humanity project, a March of Dimes walk, or a litter cleanup campaign if it affects them directly or if their peers are interested in a similar project. However, they may see little relationship between these endeavors and the larger notions of peace, hunger, or poverty and their political overtones. Of course, they are never more critical than when they see adults engage in hypocrisy. They quickly see beyond the words that are spoken to the actions that result.

Not all adolescents check the map consistently, and some are incapable of reading it. Some see the map as disjointed lines with no connection to reality. Others may see it as a general plan, certainly capable of a thousand alterations as the journey proceeds. Those more clearly focused youth seek out every detail of the map to be certain that they will reach their destination. Many, unsure of their destination, are baffled at every juncture. Intellectual development and academic endeavors take very divergent paths for adolescents. Some are more capable of academic success than others. Some will leave the map behind and never look at it again, choosing instead to follow their own direction. Some will discard it today but search it out tomorrow. Some will forget that they have a map. And others will clutch the map tightly, following a direct path to their destination.

ADOLESCENTS AT THE CROSSROAD: EMOTIONAL DEVELOPMENT

As adolescents continue their journey, they reach the crossroad of emotional development. Some will argue that emotions predominate in adolescence. In early adolescence, this is certainly true. As teens move into middle and late adolescence, the other stages of development take on more significance. Decisions that adolescents make at this crossroad have such long-term results that adults often stand on the sidelines with great trepidation. At the same time, adolescents stand at the crossroad with one hand clutching the parent and the other hand waving good-bye. Adolescents appear to send very mixed messages because they are uncertain of their own feelings. The female adolescent may be exuberant the day she is invited to the prom and in the depths of despair the next day because she is certain that she will never find the perfect dress for that occasion. The male may find it easy to express tender feelings to a new girlfriend in the morning and then engage in a fistfight with his best friend that afternoon.

Most adolescents successfully traverse the rugged terrain of this crossroad and enter adulthood as stronger travelers. However, some either become arrested at this point in their journey or leave the path entirely. Those who are arrested fail to move beyond the dependency on family. For whatever reason, they choose the safety and security of the known to the uncertainty of the unknown. They prolong the period of adolescence, remaining at home much longer than their peers. Once they do leave the security of the family, they may expect the rest of society to care for them in the same way that their parents have done. College professors, marriage partners, and even their own children may be expected to continue providing for their emotional security. Those who leave the path entirely fail to experience the depth of their dependency on their family. They may move out of the home prematurely, insisting that they have no need of a parent and the emotional security provided in that environment. Their fight for independence creates a great deal of turmoil during adolescence. These teens may also have difficulty in establishing relationships because they have not recognized their own dependency needs. Such teens may become pregnant during this push for independence, but often the pregnancy results from the desire to assert independence, rather than from a mature decision to take responsibility for another life.

The Narcissistic Stage

This push-pull relationship with parents dominates the emotional development of adolescents. Emotionally, most teens realize their dependency upon their parents. However, they are physically and intellectually capable of making many decisions on their own. They need and want to make independent decisions, yet they realize they are not yet fully capable of doing so. They want the emotional security of a safe home environment as well as the freedom to come and go as they please. So they bounce back and forth between the emotional rebellion of the young child and the tender feelings of a mature adult. They stand at the crossroad, eager to move ahead on their own but also terrified of doing so.

The Greek myth of Narcissus tells of the handsome young man who falls in love with his own reflection. In his attempt to reach the reflection in the pond, he distorts his own image. Finally, Narcissus pines away at the side of the pond. He wastes away as he gazes upon his own image. Although he has found his ultimate love, he is destroyed by it. Adolescents stand ever in danger of wasting away in the same manner on this journey as they gaze upon themselves and continually try to adjust their image to that of their expectations.

But this stage of narcissism is essential for growth and development. Teens must abandon their idolatry of the parent in order to foster their own identity. Healthy narcissism allows teens to seek approval and admiration from those they most respect. This very necessary stage of development allows them to develop independence so they will feel comfortable in breaking away from the security of the home environment. Peter Blos claims, "The process of separation and its facilitation are what give the narcissistic stage its positive and progressive quality" (Blos 1962, 92). Only by focusing on themselves are the adolescents able to establish their own identity.

The Peer Group

Of course, adolescents are incapable of establishing this identity by themselves, so they look to their peer group for reassurance. The group, the gang, the clique—all serve the same purpose. Peers provide a code of conduct, an acceptable dress code, and a language only partially understood by adults. Adolescents can thus move from the safety and security of the home to what they consider to be the safety and security of their peers. However, all the peers are involved in the same process of searching for independence. Insecure themselves, they often provide much less safety and security than the home. And because of their insecurity, they often will ostracize other teens who attempt to express their own individuality.

Contemporary adolescents also suffer from an increasing sense of isolation. Patricia Hersch spent three years attending high school and becoming intimately acquainted with students at the middle school and high school in Reston, Virginia. She summarizes her experiences in *A Tribe Apart* (1999). She calls adolescents "a tribe apart" because they are often left to their own devices, with little if any adult supervision. Adolescents often return to empty homes while their parents are out making a living, or making a life. Adolescents teach one another the skills necessary for adulthood while they are still learning the skills themselves. Hersch says it best, "The most stunning change for adolescents today is their aloneness. The adolescents of the nineties are more isolated and more unsupervised than other generations" (Hersch 1999, 19). This invisibility of adolescence merely reflects the loss of community in all of society, but it nevertheless leaves teens with an increasingly difficult emotional burden. At the time they are trying to establish independence from the adult community, there is rarely an adult community present to notice. The only conclusion we can draw is that more and more adolescents are now at risk because of lack of adult mentors. To spend more and more time alone increases the narcissism. While narcissism is a necessary phase of development, it should not be a permanent state. Those who continue in this state of self-absorption make poor spouses, irresponsible employees, and unreliable parents.

Adolescents do not complete the journey to adulthood if they become stuck in any one of the developmental stages. The emotional crossroad offers many options. The adolescent may struggle with independence and dependence, give a fond farewell to the parents, and still return home when the road gets too rough and bumpy. The adolescent may stare at his reflection in the pond for days and days. But if he remains there alone, self-absorbed by his own reflection, he runs the risk of falling into the pond and drowning. Or the adolescent may exchange the baggage of his family for the baggage of his peers and follow their lead through the dense forest, slopping through the mud and rain, ill prepared for the winter weather that lies ahead. Most adolescents will check out several of these paths before deciding which one is most appropriate for them.

TRAINING FOR THE JOURNEY: PHYSICAL DEVELOPMENT

As adolescents move along on their journey, they enter the stage of physical development. Suddenly adolescents are in the middle of the journey, absorbed with stimulation both inside and outside, and they notice that the body they now own is not the body they remember. Young adolescents are especially intrigued and dismayed with their bodies. Go into a junior high classroom sometime and notice the difference in the sizes of eighth-grade males. Some are only slightly taller than their ten-year-old brothers, and others have reached most of their adult height. It is no wonder that junior high boys are always tripping over their feet. Their feet were not nearly so long yesterday. Likewise, girls entering puberty develop breasts, which become all too obvious to both them and to their male peers. Yesterday's clothes do not fit today, and feelings about the body that were just fine last week suddenly feel very awkward.

Body Image

The most obvious differences revolve around sexual development. Wet dreams, menstrual periods, and changes in physique are constant reminders of the unpredictability of the body. Some adolescents may seek drastic measures to ensure that the situation is not permanent. Girls often develop eating disorders during this period of time. They may be dissatisfied with the extra weight gained as hips and breasts expand. If they have reasons to be upset with this new physique, they may make every attempt to return to the thin profile they had as youngsters. Girls who have had traumatic sexual experiences during this time, such as rape or incest, may be especially prone to eating disorders. The danger, of course, is that by peering into the narcissistic pond too long while trying to regain the image of youth, they may lose their very lives.

Sports Involvement

Athletic participation becomes a primary focus of many teens. Both school and community athletic programs seek the involvement of youth because they have nearly adult stature, increasing stamina, and the flexibility to develop a great deal of athletic prowess. And youth that enjoy athletics also discover that there may be many rewards for their endeavors. Scholarships, opportunities for Olympic competition, and certainly the pleasurable gazes of their peers are enough to keep many adolescents fully involved with athletic competition for years.

Sleep Needs

The down side of this physical training is the danger of sleep deprivation. Recent studies have shown that teens need more sleep at this time of their lives, yet they are less likely to get an adequate amount (Carskadon 1999). Increasing responsibilities for school, work, and athletics take their toll on youth whose bodies are still working rapidly to keep up with the demands of increased size and muscle. Ronald Dahl, M.D., indicates a correlation between sleep deprivation and the elevation of emotional difficulties. Changes in both mood and motivation result from inadequate sleep. Teens with attention deficit hyperactivity disorder also find that their symptoms increase when deprived of adequate sleep (Dahl, 1999). A small number of schools, such as those in Minnesota, now start school later in the morning to accommodate the needs of teens. Unfortunately, most high schools start school earlier than all other grade levels, in spite of the need for additional rest.

Although adolescents approximate adult size and physique by the time they leave their teens, their bodies sometimes fail to keep up with these vast changes. Full of energy, they may still lack stamina. Full of adrenaline, they may accomplish great feats yet falter under pressure. Unsure of their physical capabilities, they may push their bodies to extreme measures in an attempt to meet the competition. And many adolescents are rewarded for such endeavors. However, they may suffer long-term effects from training for the journey in this manner. Notice how many middle-aged men suffer from knee and back pain as a result of teen football injuries. The prevalence of steroid use among athletes and the dangers of weight loss among wrestlers are even more alarming. Equally frightening are the young women who train for the journey by denying themselves the nourishment necessary for growth. Their attempts to emulate skinny models often put their lives in extreme danger. Anorexia and bulimia may be cured if caught soon enough, but convincing the young woman that these habits are harmful rather than helpful may be impossible. The adolescent notion of invincibility is most clearly noted in the way they train for the journey. They may recognize that they are intellectually or emotionally vulnerable, but it is far more difficult for them to recognize that they are physically vulnerable.

A MOUNTAINTOP EXPERIENCE: SPIRITUAL DEVELOPMENT

The adolescents' final steps take them to the mountaintop of spiritual development. In many ways, these steps are the most confusing and difficult, but they may be the ones most easily ignored, as well. After all, adolescents do not even have to climb the mountain. They can go around it; they can build a tunnel through it. Why would they traverse the treacherous trail to the top of the mountain?

Faith Stages

Prior to adolescence, children usually embrace the spiritual foundations laid by their parents. James Fowler (1981) talks about the possibility of six stages of faith development. The first stage, normally experienced by children between the ages of two and seven, is an intuitive-projective faith. This stage consists of fantasy and an intrigue with stories of faith portrayed by significant persons in their lives. School-aged children usually enter stage two, the mythic-literal phase of faith development. They are particularly intrigued with stories that make them part of the community. They accept all stories literally and learn a keen sense of justice and fairness.

When adolescents start to notice the contradictory nature of the narratives and begin to question them, they move into stage three, synthetic-conventional faith. This stage of development can be seen as a process of ego development. The ego develops the capacity for tolerating a diversity of opinions at the same time that it desires a level of order that will provide a sense of security (Erikson1968).

All synthetic-conventional faith views faith in interpersonal terms; because of this perspective, adolescents expect to conform to the ideals of others. As in emotional development, the adolescent vests authority in the consensus of the valued group. However, the adolescent in stage three is very much bound to tradition and conformity, regardless of outside appearances to the contrary. Symbols become extremely important to adolescents, and in fact, the symbols themselves become sacred. Whether it is a good-luck charm or a cross, teens can become quite attached to these symbolic representations of their spirituality.

Although there are some who think that adolescents are more likely to mirror spirituality of the New Age in contemporary America, the work of Smith with Denton belies this fact. Their research confirms that most American teenagers conform to conventional religious identity and practices. They accept the spiritual views and values of their parents and assume that any changes in their beliefs will occur in their adult life. Regardless of its expression, they mirror the spiritual development they see in the rest of their society (Smith with Denton 2005).

Teens may not invite their parents to the mountaintop, although most hope to see them waving to them from the valley below. They reject parents and other authorities that assume that the future is inexplicably determined by the past. Adolescents reason that if their identification is irreversible, then they are deprived of their own identity. This rejection of parents, seen in almost every phase of their development, is a rejection of such a deterministic view. Although children's original concept of God is very much determined by their concept of their parents, they eventually will separate the two (Knight 1967). In struggling for freedom and independence, adolescents may reject either God or parents—or sometimes both. However, as they work through this rebellion, they may arrive at a new understanding of God that may be more personally meaningful.

Of course, there are pitfalls along the way. Some adolescents never get to the mountaintop. A break in interpersonal relationships along the way may cause the teen to abandon his journey. The trip up the mountain may in fact be too difficult if he has to make the trip alone. On the other hand, he may make a more concerted effort to reach the top of the mountain, focusing rigidly on the destination. His determination may result in an unwavering faith, boxed in by even more rigid rules than those imposed by his own family and faith tradition. Along the way, he may meet others on a similar pilgrimage. If they provide a clear code of conduct, he may follow them without question. Notice the influence of religious cults and urban gangs on this age group.

Adolescents in stage three are committed to values and images without examining them. Some adults remain in this stage of faith development for the remainder of their lives. However, other experiences may cause adolescents to move ahead in their spiritual journey. Adolescent experiences that may cause more serious reflection include clashes between valued sources of authority, marked changes in persons or practices that they viewed as sacred, or engaging in new experiences such as leaving home (Fowler 1981). In recent years, adolescents have been more subject to these kinds of experiences. Parents are more likely to clash with authorities such as the church and the government, leaving youth to wonder which authority has the superior position. Recent disclosures of sexual philandering among the priesthood may have an even more profound effect upon spiritual development of the young. Since most adolescents eventually have a variety of experiences and leave home in the process of this exploration, many will begin to question their spiritual beliefs and practices. If they do so, they may move ahead to stage four, individuative-reflective faith. This stage normally occurs in late adolescence, when individuals separate themselves from the group and establish their own worldview. This stage involves critical reflection and the ability to demythologize the faith stories (Fowler 1981).

No matter what their skin color, faith background, or cultural understanding, adolescents are in search of something greater than themselves. Their own egos are so fragile that they must believe in something in order to continue the journey. They may just harbor a belief that the mountaintop exists; they may hold tenaciously to the belief that God loves them unconditionally; they may believe that once they get to the mountaintop, the fog will clear and they can see forever. Regardless, they need to hold onto the past at the same time they trudge recklessly into the future. They want a path to follow, even if it is strewn with debris left carelessly by earlier pilgrims.

THE JOURNEY CONTINUES

The journey never ends, of course. Adolescents think it ends when they reach adulthood. They think their cares, their burdens, and their frustrations will lighten with each step along the way. Yes, they will eventually have a clearer notion of their intellectual capabilities. They either will or will not continue with their academic endeavors. Someone along the way will either encourage or discourage them, and if unsure about their own capabilities, they will probably believe those adults. They will eventually feel more secure unless the journey damaged them too much. They will eventually learn that few people were actually looking at them all the time anyway. And those few who were looking were probably seeing a lot more potential than the adolescent imagined. Most will emerge from the mirror-like reflection of the pond more like themselves than like Narcissus. Some will continue to glory in the physical prowess of their youth. Others will abandon it or substitute other meaningful activities. And many will get at least a small glimpse of the mountaintop. They may not get there until after a broken relationship, a life-threatening illness, or the loss of a loved one. They may stay on the mountaintop awhile, but eventually, they continue on the journey. After all, it is only the beginning of a lifelong odyssey.

REFERENCES

Blos, P. 1962. *On Adolescence*. New York: The Free Press.

Carskadon, M. A. 1999. "When Worlds Collide." *Phi Delta Kappan*. 80 (5): 348–353.

Dahl, R. E. 1999. "The Consequences of Insufficient Sleep for Adolescents." *Phi Delta Kappan*. 80 (5): 354–359.

Erikson, E. H. 1968. *Identity: Youth and Crisis*. New York: W. W. Norton and Company.

Fowler, J. W. 1981. *Stages of Faith: The Psychology of Human Development and the Quest for Meaning*. San Francisco: Harper and Row.

Gilligan, C. 1982. *In a Different Voice*. Cambridge: Harvard University Press.

Hersch, P. 1999. *A Tribe Apart*. New York: Ballantine Books.

Knight, J. A. 1967. "Religious-Psychological Conflicts of the Adolescent. " In *Adolescence: Care and Counseling*, edited by Gene Usdin, 31–50. Philadelphia: J. B. Lippincott Company.

Kohlberg, L. 1984. *The Psychology of Moral Development*. San Francisco: Harper and Row.

Piaget, J. 1981. *Intelligence and Affectivity*. Palo Alto, CA Annual Reviews Inc.

Schneider, B., and D. Stevenson. 1999. *The Ambitious Generation*. New Haven, CT: Yale University Press.

Smith, C., with M. L. Denton. 2005. *Soul Searching*. New York: Oxford University Press.

2

ENJOYING THE JOURNEY

If you picked this book off the shelf, chances are that you did so because you are either working with youth or preparing to work with youth in some significant helping capacity. Because of your very special relationship to teens, you will accompany them on significant parts of their adolescent journey. You also sincerely like these young people and enjoy their slang, their idealism, and their overwhelming enthusiasm. Of course, you will accompany them through their many mood swings, their troubled sexual relationships, and their family issues as you join this trek. But if you truly like this rather confusing stage of growth, teens will like you as well, and your relationships will become exceptionally meaningful.

However, those of us employed to work with teens realize that we have many other audiences to which we are responsible. Obviously, because these youth are minors, we have a responsibility to relate to their parents, and that relationship can be a bit tricky because teens are establishing their independence from the family. Nevertheless, this relationship is still a key component of their growth. They will mirror the family in most of their relationships, and when a crisis occurs, the parents must be notified. It is not easy to notify parents that their teen is suicidal or homicidal, but the law requires that we do so, and because we care about these young charges, we must notify the adults who are legally responsible for them. In the same manner, if youth are being abused or are engaged in abuse, the legal authorities must be notified.

And the legal system is only one of many entities that will tell professionals what they must do and how they must do it. Many of you will be employed by agencies that will tell you what your goals and objectives must be. They will set strict guidelines about what you must accomplish, how you must measure your effectiveness, and when and where your reports will be filed. At times, the paperwork and bureaucracy may seem rather daunting. But in the midst of all the requirements, there is usually a large degree of flexibility regarding the ways in which you can relate to the adolescents under your care. Since you chose to work with adolescents because you truly enjoy them, read on to see how to make the journey even more enjoyable while you continue to meet all the requirements of your government or private agency.

CLEARING THE TRAIL

If an agency employed you to work with youth, they did so because they felt that you had something to offer this group of teens. You were not employed simply to listen to their music, hang out with them, or engage in their self-centered conversations, although at times you may be doing all of those things. You were employed because you could offer some sort of educational benefit to these teens. You are the one who is to guide them in clearing the trail. In doing so, you are preparing them for their adult responsibilities, whether in the workplace, the family structure, or the community at large.

You may be working with youth in a school or other educational setting. If that is the case, your primary role is to prepare youth to be productive members of society. You are charged with providing the proper academic background so that they may become members of the workforce. You may further be charged with assisting them in their relationships with peers, family members, and authority figures. You are responsible to the state for reaching the state standards, providing accountability to prove that students have met those standards, and reporting any deficiencies. You are further responsible to your principal, headmaster, or some other administrator, and you are responsible to a school board or board of directors.

On the other hand, you may have been hired by a prevention agency. If so, you are probably working with youth to prevent further involvement in the court or legal system, to prevent drug and alcohol abuse, or to otherwise intervene in situations where youth are likely to be at risk. You are also likely to be responsible to the state or federal government for meeting grant guidelines, including the ability to prove that your program is effective in meeting its stated objectives. You may have been handed a program listed as a "best practice" and told to follow its guidelines to success. You may have received a lot of training by your supervisor, or you may have received very little training in this area. But if you cannot meet your stated objectives, your job or your funding will disappear. So you, too, are under considerable pressure to clear the trail for all youth under your supervision.

If you are working for a mental health agency, you may have a bit more flexibility in terms of the ways in which you structure your involvement with youth. But you must meet insurance guidelines, keep up-to-date on treatment plans, and satisfy a board of directors. You may have some of the same strictures as a prevention agency because of grant guidelines required by the government.

If you are self-employed, you probably have more flexibility than any of these other scenarios. But if you do not satisfy the customer (the youth) and the payroll clerk (the parent or insurance provider), you will not be employed very long. If you are in this situation, you likely have considerably more experience and are willing to take the risk to follow your own dreams, as well as those of the youth in your care.

All of you have the right and the responsibility to enjoy this journey with the youth in your care. Drama can be used to meet the outcomes designated by you or the audiences to whom you are responsible. It can also make the journey all the more pleasurable. After all, you came into this line of work because you truly loved it. Neither the state nor any other supervisory agency will be able to destroy your enthusiasm.

ENGINEERS WHO DESIGNED THE TRAIL

Whether we call them risk and protective factors, developmental assets, or resiliency, every professional who works with youth is trying to improve the life situation of youth and give them the skills they need to be successful adults. Considerable research has taken place over the last two decades to determine what positive benefits could be afforded to our youth and children. The emphasis shifted from simply overcoming problems to building the assets that could assist all youth and children throughout their development.

Bonnie Benard (1991) compiled considerable research in the field of resiliency. Her research revealed similar protective factors that can be provided by the family, the school, and the community. The three areas complement one another, but Benard also recognized that strengths in any one of the three areas can overcome deficits in the others. Intervention attempts to shift the balance from risk to resiliency, either by decreasing the risks or increasing the protective factors. Sometimes even just one good experience may make all the difference in the life of a child. The school and community can provide those protective factors.

Resilient youth exemplify social competence, problem-solving skills, autonomy, and a sense of purpose and future. Socially competent youth are responsive, flexible, empathic, and caring. They also have good communication skills and a sense of humor. Youth with good problem-solving skills can think abstractly, flexibly, and reflectively. They can also see alternate solutions to complex problems. Autonomous youth may sometimes be described as those with good self-esteem. They have an internal locus of control and are self-disciplined. Because resilient youth have a sense of purpose and future, they have educational goals, and those goals are far more important than their academic achievement. Families, schools and communities can all work together to provide youth with these resiliency factors (Benard 1991).

The Search Institute has conducted considerable research into developmental assets, those positive assets that help youth become healthy adults. Research in communities around the United States identified forty assets that can be provided by the home and community. The work of Benson, Galbraith, and Espeland (1995) divides thirty of these assets into sixteen external assets and fourteen internal assets. Parents provide the structure for most of the external assets, including such things as parental discipline and monitoring, parental involvement in school, a faith community, and extracurricular activities. The internal assets include attitudes and values of the child. Many of these assets can be taught or reinforced by the community. They include such assets as empathy, assertiveness skills, planning skills, and decision-making skills. According to the recent work by Scales and Leffert (2004), the average adolescent exemplifies fewer than half of these forty assets. The heartening thing about their research is the knowledge that with adolescents, protective factors are far more influential than risk factors with regard to long-term effects.

As mentioned earlier, the goal of prevention programs, as well as the goal of many intervention programs, is to change the balance between risk and protective factors. The National Institute on Drug Abuse (2003) has made it clear that programs that aim to deter drug and alcohol use must increase protective factors so they outweigh the risk factors. The work on risk and protective factors is considerable. We shall examine only those particular risk and protective factors that have the most bearing on the programs you are likely to be running.

Those youth most likely to abuse drugs have a high number of risk factors and a low number of protective factors. They also suffer from high stress, poor parental support, and poor academic competence. The lack of support from a caring adult family member is a significant factor for much at-risk behavior. Risk factors that are likely to be seen in the school and community include aggression and impulsivity, poor coping skills, association with peers engaged in problematic behavior, and a perception that drug and alcohol use is acceptable among their peers and in their community. The key risk periods for drug and alcohol abuse occur at times of transition, such as puberty, moving, and divorce. Transitions from to middle school and to high school are also periods of high risk (National Institute on Drug Abuse 2003).

Protective factors such as parental monitoring of behavior, success in academic and extracurricular activities, and strong bonds with positive institutions can combine with norms that oppose drug abuse. These factors can go a long way in building resiliency even among the most at-risk youth. There are several key protective factors that can also decrease substance use so that it does not escalate to substance abuse. The community can provide some of these, but it cannot provide all of them. The key factors are self-control, protective family structure, the individual personality, and environmental variables. But most importantly, interventions that provide skills and support to these at-risk youth can both increase the protective factors and prevent drug abuse (National Institute on Drug Abuse 2003).

SHELTER FOR THE JOURNEY

Your role as group facilitator is a vital and important one. Research continues to validate and stress the importance of caring and support in the life of a child. Just as a shelter provides relief from the burning heat, the vicissitudes of weather, and natural predators, so, too, may significant adults provide protection from the storm of adolescence. And in this place of safety, time can be spent in rejuvenating efforts to rebuild or create the protective factors for the remainder of the journey. Adults outside the family play a critical role in providing a sense of well-being for teens (Scales and Leffert 2004). The business of care and support also requires an environment that will provide social bonding, led by adults who will relate to them with high expectations and give them the opportunity for active participation.

In the school, caring staff and peers may provide that support. In fact, Benard (1991) determined that peer programs of helpful support were found to be the very best school approach to decrease alcohol and other drug use. However, recent research indicates negative outcomes when high-risk youth are placed in the same peer group, since they apparently reinforce negative behaviors and substance abuse (National Institute on Drug Abuse 2003). Schools may also provide high expectations and assist students in internalizing those expectations. They work with youth to become involved in responsible roles that require problem solving, decision making, and goal setting, elements essential for the resilient child (Benard 1991).

Family and community are equally important in providing the care and support for youth. The community often relies upon helping professionals such as you to assist with this process. Essential to this involvement is the need for youth to bond with others and the chance for them to gain control over their own lives. Those elements involve cooperation, dialogue, and empathy. The community that provides such care and support will also provide human services such as health and childcare, housing, recreation, and employment. Because this community values high expectations, it values youth as a valuable resource, recognizing that youth will also reflect the community values, and it encourages teens to participate in useful tasks that contribute to the welfare of that community (Benard 1991).

TOOLS FOR THE JOURNEY

You may well be saying at this point, "Okay, so now I know why I need to work with youth and what they need to be successful, but how will I do it?" You may have a group showing up at your doorstep or classroom door shortly, and you need to have specific ways to approach them successfully. The research gives specific suggestions about the types of interventions that are most likely to be successful with youth.

Whether you are teaching in a school setting or working in the prevention or intervention field, your goal is one of help and support for youth. If you are in a school program, prevention efforts should be integrated into academic performance to increase the bond with school and decrease the likelihood of dropping out. In that environment you can more effectively address the misperception that most students are abusing drugs and alcohol.

The basis of any effective prevention program for youth involves these three core elements:

1. structure
2. content
3. delivery.

Even if your drug or other prevention content is accurate and up-to-date, this information alone has proven to be ineffective. It is far better to combine information with specific skills development that may lead to a change in behavior. Some examples would include improving communication in the family, improving academic and social competence, building social skills, and peer resistance strategies. Furthermore, using interactive methods will reinforce the prevention content (National Institute on Drug Abuse 2003). "It has been documented, across cultures, that cognitive development is greatly enhanced through social interactions" (Wood 1997,152).

Interactive Techniques

When we examine a few of the internal developmental assets, and the suggestions for their instruction, we see further reinforcement for this idea of interactive methods. Benson, Galbraith, and Espeland (1995) mention the use of interactive techniques in the instruction of the following assets: empathy, assertiveness, decision making, and friendship building. For example, one can assist youth in developing empathy by teaching conflict resolution skills, encouraging talk about feelings, and exposing students to the experiences of others. Both role-playing and visualization work toward those ends. Assertiveness can be taught by modeling and role-playing, in which the facilitator encourages youth to stand up for themselves and express their own beliefs. Youth may practice decision making by using experiential activities so they can make difficult decisions in a less threatening situation where adults may guide them through the process. Friendship building also occurs more naturally in an interactive environment that celebrates diversity.

The words *interaction* and *role-playing* keep coming up in all the research about effective programming. What could be more interactive than drama itself? Even the prevention experts like Scales and Leffert (2004) state the importance of role-playing likely scenarios that teens will encounter. Such scenes and following discussion will allow them to improve their decision-making skills and reinforce the concepts. Drama by its very nature demands concentration, imagination, teamwork, and empathy. Although role-playing is often the only form of drama included in prevention programs, drama can go far beyond the simple role-playing format to involve more youth in meaningful growth activities. And at the same time, drama can be used to meet state standards, assessment needs, and a variety of outcomes that might be imposed by any governmental or private agency.

DRAMA VERSUS THEATRE

Let us be clear that we are talking about the incorporation of drama, not theatre. Every individual is born with the potential for drama, and every individual participates in drama, from the early years in which playing is simply the acting out of a story or one's favorite characters, to the times in adult life when one pretends to be what an employer wants in an interview. Drama, by its very nature, is communication between participants. Theatre is communication between performers and an audience. Also, drama may be taught in a workshop atmosphere, while theatre usually culminates in performance (Erickson 1992). Brian Way reminds us

> Here again is the difference between theatre and drama; schools do not exist to develop actors, but to develop people, and one of the major factors in developing people is that of preserving and enriching to its fullest the human capacity to give a full and undivided attention to any matter in hand at any given moment. (Way 1967, 15)

And all efforts at prevention could benefit from this teaching of concentration, not simply those efforts put forth in the school setting.

Building Concentration

Concentration is essential for any age group and for any situation. But it is especially important to adolescents because of their self-consciousness. When teens are convinced that everyone is looking at them, it becomes more difficult to concentrate on someone else or a task at hand. By providing a structure that demands concentration, we are giving everyone a chance to truly listen to each other, increasing the opportunities for youth to learn more about themselves (Wood 1997). And drama demands that kind of concentration. It is not possible to react to another person until you have truly heard, seen, and felt what the other is experiencing.

But you need not call what you will be doing drama. In fact, because youth may associate the word *drama* with the theatre, they may well assume that they are incapable of participating if they have not yet stood on the stage and been applauded by an audience. And you, as a facilitator, may be hesitant if you have not been professionally trained in the theatre. Since the desire to play is innate in all of us, you may incorporate any number of playful techniques into your group experiences.

You are probably aware of many arts-in-the-schools programs that attempt to build bridges between the classroom and the world of the fine arts. Those programs are highly successful, but they depend upon outside funding and the availability of professional artists. Many of those programs, such as the ArtsPartners (Reardon 2005) program in Dallas, attempt to integrate academic work with artistic endeavors. They have notable results in promoting literacy. Similar programs in the prevention field have linked professional artists with prevention programs quite successfully. The authors have no desire to discount any of those highly effective programs, whether instituted by the school district or local prevention agencies. Such interdisciplinary endeavors are to be highly commended. But we wish to suggest that you may incorporate many fine drama techniques into your own educational or prevention group using the techniques presented here. These techniques involve minimal expense and can be used to meet state guidelines in every academic subject from the language arts to social studies and health. We have even seen professional educators teach math skills using a dramatic format. Drama can always be incorporated in teaching interpersonal skills, and almost everyone who works with teens is asked to address that issue.

The Circle Dash Game

Since we recognize the importance of concentration in everything from sports to academia, the techniques will speak for themselves. For example, you might start a group using the Circle Dash game (Rohd 1998). One person stands in the middle of a circle. Everyone else stands around him. His goal is to get a place in the circle. The goal of other participants is to switch places by communicating to others in the group, without speaking.

Participants may wink or otherwise signal to another group member their desire to switch places. The person in the middle will try to catch the signal and get to the place before the switch occurs. Several persons may switch places at the same time. The game provides great opportunities for concentration, as well as the expenditure of great bursts of energy.

Engaging Imagination

If teens are to learn decision making and goal setting, they also have to develop an imagination. Of course, everyone is born with imagination, but by the time a child reaches adolescence, we have often relegated imagination to a study of the fine arts, to be used only in art, music, or theatre classes. Way (1967) reminds us that imagination is part of life itself and can be incorporated into all aspects of a person's learning. Imagination is that ability to see something in the mind's eye. It can be enhanced with appropriate techniques that encourage even the most hesitant teens to engage themselves in the process.

Using Visualization Techniques

Visualization techniques work well for engaging the mind. When facilitators set the scene, they give only minimal instructions, allowing all group participants to build their story according to their own needs. Visualization exercises can be useful in helping teens to see the future and set goals by allowing them to see into the unknown. For example, the facilitator might ask teens to imagine themselves ten years into the future. As they close their eyes, the facilitator guides the process, asking them to see where they are living, what they are using for transportation, the ways in which they spend their waking hours, and the people they associate with. A visualization exercise such as this one could focus on career goals, lifestyle choices, or educational goals. The facilitator must lead the visualization in a calm, soothing voice and avoid the insertion of a great number of details so that teens can fill in those specifics themselves.

Creating Teamwork

Community building requires the development of teamwork skills. We are well aware of athletic teams who lose because of lack of teamwork, employees who lose their jobs because of an inability to work with their colleagues, and community groups that fail because of a lack of clear understanding among group members. If you want your group to succeed and work together, teamwork must take place. What better way to work toward that end than incorporating drama into your group work? The group must work together to create a scene, tell a story, or communicate an idea.

There are numerous group activities in this book that serve as wonderful teambuilding exercises. Here's one to whet your appetite.

The Human Machine Exercise

You may assign a theme to this machine if you like. It could be a machine that creates a specific feeling, such as trust, hope, or joy. It could be a machine of a healthy body, a progressive government, or a tyrant. At any rate, once you decide upon the role of the machine, ask group members to come one at a time to join this machine. As in any working machine, all parts should have a function, and they should relate to each other in some way. Group members need not touch each other, but they need to show by the rhythm established that they are related to other parts of the machine. Later, if you like, group members can add a sound, word, or phrase that their part of the machine might emit. Be sure to discuss afterwards how group members felt as a part of the machine, and be prepared for some to say that they felt silly. Teens ask for this activity to be repeated over and over again, so be prepared to vary it slightly with each endeavor.

Developing Empathy

How could you possibly work to develop empathy in the hearts and minds of teenagers? Yes, teens are self-centered and narcissistic, but they also like attention, even if they shun it at times. Adults can use that bid for attention to their advantage by incorporating drama into their groups. They can then use that emotional pull by working with teens to develop a sense of how someone else might feel. If you clearly establish early in the group that you are asking teens to make up a story, tell how something might happen, and imagine how someone else might feel, you are on your way to success. However, if you ask them to tell their story, tell how something actually happened to them, and tell how they feel, the process is much more threatening. But in the process of building a story and enacting it, teens must take on the role of persons sometimes quite different from themselves. If they are to make the character believable, they must clearly reveal those thoughts and actions in a manner that the other group members will accept as realistic. Doubling and role reversal are two very effective ways to develop empathy for others (see Chapter 3).

Mirroring

A simple exercise to begin with is a mirroring one. Divide the group into pairs. One person starts the action, and the other person mirrors it. You might start with something simple like preparing for school in the morning. The second person must mirror every movement, every gesture, and every facial expression while remaining silent. Then ask the partners to reverse roles so that the first person is now mirroring the second person. Eventually

One technique for developing empathy is the mirroring exercise.

expand the situation so that the two persons are following each other without one specifically assigned as leader. You may repeat this exercise using a variety of situations for a variety of purposes. It's quite an old standby, and one that teens can profit from immensely.

TAKING THE FIRST STEP

The trail is before you. The teens are ready to embark. You have the walking stick and compass. Remember that your role is to get teens involved in structured activities under your leadership, set clear boundaries, nurture a commitment to learning, provide support and care, and encourage healthy values and concern for other persons (Benson, Galbraith, and Espeland 1995).

By incorporating drama into your structured activities with youth, you can meet the goals of your organization and have fun as well. Use that narcissism of adolescence to your advantage. Since teens think that everyone is looking at them anyway, allow the entire group to focus on itself as they create the drama. If they are convinced that they are telling a fictional story, they will tell you more truth than you might ever imagine. And if that history lesson becomes more alive when students actually become those historical personages, if the health lesson has a more lasting effect because teens had the chance to see how it feels when a nonverbal message speaks louder than a verbal one, and if the group becomes more cohesive when dealing with issues of grief and loss, you have accomplished far more than any state standard or grant requirement will demand of you. Your impact will be much more long-lasting, and you and the teens you work with will have added many pleasant memories to your journey together.

REFERENCES

Benard, B. 1991. *Fostering Resiliency in Kids: Protective Factors in the Family, School, and Community.* Portland, OR: Northwest Regional Educational Laboratory.

Benson, P. L., J. Galbraith, and P. Espeland. 1995. *What Kids Need to Succeed.* Minneapolis: Free Spirit Publishing Inc.

Erickson, K. 1992. *Getting Started with Drama.* Evanston, IL: Creative Directions.

National Institute on Drug Abuse. 2003. *Preventing Drug Use among Children and Adolescents.* Second Edition. Bethesda, MD: U.S. Department of Health and Human Services.

Reardon, C. 2005, Winter. "Deep in the Arts of Texas." *Ford Foundation Report.* Retrieved from www.fordfound.org/publications/ff_report /view_ff_detail.cfm?report_index=549.

Rohd, M. 1998. *Theatre for Community, Conflict & Dialogue.* Portsmouth, NH: Heinemann.

Scales, P. C., and N. Leffert. 2004. *Developmental Assets: A Synthesis of the Scientific Research on Adolescent Development.* Second Edition. Minneapolis: Search Institute.

Way, B. 1967. *Development Through Drama.* Amherst, NY: Humanity Books.

Wood, C. 1997. *Yardsticks: Children in the Classroom Ages 4–14.* Greenfield, MA: Northeast Foundation for Children.

3

GUIDING THE JOURNEY

The adolescent journey appears to be as much a necessity as a desire. Knowing that they will all too soon settle into a sedentary lifestyle, youth engage in wandering to enrich their own experiences. This journey encourages greater flexibility and fosters survival skills (Jennings 1995). Youth will engage with a variety of people along their way. Their ability to interact with those sojourners will, in many instances, determine their future success.

Those helping professionals who spend their lives working with adolescents have a very special task. Educators and other helping professionals often serve as tour guides for the journey. Their role is much more complex than that of a friend and much less threatening than that of the parent. Constantly on the lookout for danger, adventure, and opportunity, they coach, cajole, and sometimes even constrain the young adventurers. Walking alongside the youth, they tenuously feel their way along the rocky path, sometimes stepping aside to watch the youth venture forth alone, occasionally assisting the youth in forging a new path, and often reveling in the joy of discovering hidden treasures along the route.

The tour guide can be of special significance as an interaction guide. The primary activity of adolescence is social interaction. The emotional involvement in these interactions may at times overwhelm the adolescent, but the tour guide may help the adolescent practice healthy interactions. Helping professionals constantly work at preparing youth for their own independent lives, knowing that their ability to interact with others will often determine whether they become productive citizens and contented adults.

DRAMA USE WITH ADOLESCENTS

Drama can be especially helpful to adolescents because it allows individuals to practice interactions, engage in problem solving, and foster creative skills. Helping professionals can provide a safe environment where youth can test their choices before actually having to face the real situation (Jennings 1995). Drama also offers opportunities for youth to interact with a variety of persons. Whether those persons are real or fictional is less significant than the impact of the interaction itself. Youth must, of course, learn to distinguish between reality and fantasy, but playing in both worlds will increase the adolescent's spontaneity. The helping professional can guide the journey while affirming the value of each individual.

The Process of the Drama

Change is facilitated through the process of the drama itself. For this reason, a variety of dramatic techniques may be employed. Some may choose to use scripted plays; many will choose theatre games and improvisational techniques. Others may engage group members in the creation of masks that can tell their own unique stories. Participants may move back and forth between the roles of performer and audience, engaging in active listening, empathy, and performance skills.

All forms of theatre exist within clear boundaries. However, the typical theatrical performance exists for the sake of the performance itself. Actors learn their lines, engage themselves in their characters, and portray the action in a believable fashion. All these techniques enable the audience to more clearly assess the situation and identify with the thoughts and feelings of the drama. The actors clearly distinguish between themselves as persons and themselves as characters, knowing that they are engaged in fantasy when on the stage. Drama, as it is used in the context of the group process, however, concerns itself with the process of the dramatic interaction. The drama engages persons with real conflicts, solving real problems, for the sake of personal enlightenment. Facilitators do not assume that only good actors may participate. Nor do they assume that only scripted lines are valid. Participants will engage in drama for the sake of personal enlightenment, the joy of the spontaneous experience, and the expansion of the creative experience. A stage may or may not be used; costumes may or may not be employed; props may or may not be handled. The lack of facilities and materials rarely limits the effectiveness of a drama experience, since the most important work occurs in the process of the drama itself. The imagination of the group members will supply any missing elements.

Drama encourages youth to move back and forth between fantasy and reality. Since the engagement in fantasy is both more enjoyable and less threatening than the reality of talking about their personal issues, youth more readily enter into the process. As individuals move into the space, they may leave behind their normal cares and concerns, but even in this realm of fantasy, real issues will arise. Robert Landy states it best.

> Conversely, even the most outrageous fiction, once committed to story form, contains some grain of truth as it relates in some basic way to the imagination of the storyteller. (Landy 1993b, 31)

But because youth are asked to create a piece of fiction, portray fictional characters, and resolve fictional conflicts, they can enter the dramatic experience with more abandon. In that abandon, persons become free to make sense of a not-so-sensible world. Only after the experience is complete are they asked to reflect back upon the relationship between the fantasy and reality. And always, they are given the freedom to share only what feels comfortable in that environment.

The Group Experience

The drama process most commonly exists as a group experience, where live interaction can be both experienced and processed. Many group facilitators have experimented with traditional role-playing. Their experiences might have been highly successful or totally disastrous. The outlines in this chapter go far beyond traditional role-playing, which sometimes is too threatening early in the group experience. The authors challenge youth workers and professionals to follow the guidelines in this chapter to enliven every group. The group process must engage group members from the onset, making it comfortable for them to risk themselves. If youth are unprepared or feel vulnerable too soon, they are likely to railroad this entire process.

Traditionally, the group experience consists of three parts

1. warm-up
2. enactment
3. sharing.

Warm-up Stage

In the warm-up, participants engage in playful activities that bring the group back together and in touch with both themselves and other members of the group. Group facilitators must consider the objectives of the group experience when deciding upon which warm-up activities would be most effective for each specific session. Chapter 4 outlines a number of successful warm-up exercises, but they cannot necessarily be interchanged. Choose the ones that are most appropriate for the group, its goals, and its experiences.

Some groups will never move past the warm-up stage. The number of sessions, the intimacy of the group, and the experience of the facilitator will have a great deal of bearing upon this process. Facilitators that are new to the drama process might begin with simple warm-ups as a way of bringing the group together. The energy provided by these exercises will add immensely to the success and interactions of the group.

Enactment Stage

During the enactment phase, group members participate in the dramatic experience itself. Such activities as the sharing of monologues, the presentation of improvised scenes, and the telling of stories might take place during this phase of the session. Keep in mind that the group is dealing with fictional stories, objective realities, and impersonal truths. The reason many facilitators shy away from drama is because they are fearful of opening up emotional wounds that they may not be able to heal. The authors are not suggesting that facilitators deal with personal stories, personal wounds, or personal tragedies. A story about someone else's struggles can carry as much weight as the teen's individual struggle, but teens are never as vulnerable if they are telling someone else's story.

Sharing Stage

While the enactment phase may be the most exciting and perhaps the most insightful, no session is complete without providing a time for sharing. During this final phase, group members might share ways in which the enactment related to their own experiences, other possible ways in which the enactment might have been portrayed, or some insight about what they have learned in the process of this session. Facilitators should begin with objective questions about the enactment. Then they can move into more subjective questions that will facilitate sharing of feelings. The sharing time is not a time to praise the acting ability of participants or reward them for their dramatic skills. All participants are considered worthy of participation in the dramatic process.

The Move Toward Transformation

The process works something like this: a life experience is enacted; others respond to the experience; persons build a relationship between their life experiences and the enactment. Participants move back and forth between the roles of participant and observer. They bring their own experiences and feelings into the enactment almost unconsciously before they consciously reflect upon the impact of the enactment. Ideally, the process moves from the "dramatic projection," where the participants encounter problems in a dramatic form, to transformation, where actual changes result from the drama (Jones 1996). Mask work is especially popular with adolescents. Teens might be asked to prepare masks of public and private selves, of heroes and villains, or favorite characters from literature or history. After the masks are prepared, they then write a monologue for each character. In so doing, they are enacting a life experience. They move back and forth between the role of participant and observer as they both share their monologues and listen to the monologues of others. Participants are encouraged to respond to the experiences of their colleagues.

As the process unfolds, group members are encouraged to link the dramatic experience with that of their own lives. Transformation, or change in perspective, is the goal of any group. That process of transformation may sometimes be seen during the process of the group work. On the other hand, the transformation

Mask work with adolescent groups can help individuals gain new perspectives.

may occur at some later date. However, the facilitator and participants are much better prepared to see the possibilities of change
in the dramatic format.

And why does it work? Landy claims, "Improvisation is in
many ways a form of adult play" (Landy 1993b, 18). Probably that

is the key. Adolescents have only recently left behind the toys, playmates, and fantasies of their childhood. The wise guide knows that to work effectively with adolescents, one must appeal to their adult thoughts and dreams without regressing to childish activities. Adolescents are too close to enjoy the reckless abandon of childhood, and they covet the freedoms of the adult world. Improvisation allows the intellect to function while still appealing to the creativity of the artistic experience.

The expressive arts have performed an unconscious healing function throughout the history of the world. The group facilitator can harness that same energy and bring it to a conscious state. In the process of restoring balance, the joy of play and the comfort of ritual can be employed to bring about conscious change (Landy 1993a). In such a process, feelings and thoughts can be more easily expressed than when they are addressed in a more direct, less metaphorical manner. For instance, it is often difficult to address sensitive issues with teens early in the group experience. But the authors have discovered that youth will readily participate in an artistic exercise that allows them to explore issues in a more personal sense. Graphic images often bypass verbal censorship, allowing a fuller expression of both thoughts and feelings. Following the artistic exercise, teens can be encouraged to tell a story, write a monologue, or create a dialogue about the graphic image. The facilitator provides the environment, encourages participation, and joins in sharing with the group. The repetitious nature of the warm-up, enactment, and sharing provide the ritual function, giving a sense of both safety and security to the environment.

While drama may be appropriately used with a variety of age groups, it is especially significant for adolescents because it encourages active involvement in the creative process. Drama, by its very nature, is an interactive, social process. Since adolescents expend most of their emotional and physical energy in the process of socialization, drama fits well with their developmental process. Note how often adolescents will retell a story with "he said" then "she said," certain to include all the dynamics of the interaction.

As youth engage in the group process, they learn to overcome their narcissistic tendencies. They learn that their problems are universal, reducing their sense of alienation. The intense interaction of the group process appeals to the adolescent's need to belong. And by engaging in that process, they develop empathy. Renee Emunah states, "Even more important than the experience of acceptance is that of empathy. The live enactments in drama therapy communicate nuance and feeling in such a way that empathy is heightened" (Emunah 1995, 161). Acting closely corresponds with adolescent behavior because it is action-oriented and spontaneous, rather than simply a verbal experience. Adolescent experiences, language, and actions can be presented in a safe environment, and the adolescents can be rewarded for their creative endeavors.

DEVELOPMENTAL WORK OF DRAMA

Drama meets many of the needs of adolescents as they proceed along their journey. However, their participation must be considered meaningful and worthy of adult praise. The Acting Out troupe of adolescents in New Hampshire was once introduced as a group of children performing skits. Their facilitators, when writing their own text, toyed with the subtext, "We Are Not Children, and We Do Not Do Skits" (Cossa et al. 1996, 3). Adolescents want to deal with real issues, and those issues often include the serious ones, such as teen pregnancy, suicide, abuse, and violence. Portrayals of such issues cannot rightfully be called "skits." Skits provide entertainment and amusement. Teens who engage in drama do so in order to work through issues of importance. They are wrongfully served if their work is treated simply as childish entertainment.

Drama as Intervention

The storminess of adolescence can be addressed in many fashions. Trusted adults choose to accompany the youth through the storm. If interventions are offered for troubled adolescents, the storm is less likely to cause permanent damage, and the storm itself may become a positive element of that growth. By providing a non-threatening and constructive environment, helping professionals can provide an opportunity to assist communication and reduce alienation. Drama and other creative arts are appropriate interventions because they allow for the intense and sometimes chaotic emotions of adolescence to be expressed outside of the self. Many youth develop a high degree of creativity at this time in their development, and their aesthetic sensibilities take on a conceptual framework at this time in their lives (Emunah 1995).

Putting the emotions and chaos into a fictional drama allows the adolescent to establish some distance from the perceived problem. Drama becomes a safe container for thoughts, feelings, and experiences that might otherwise appear quite threatening. Dramatic distance allows youth to engage in problem solving that is less of a personal risk. It is much easier for youth to change the outcome of a story than for those same teens to make major changes in their own behavior. Furthermore, the helping professional can inquire about general concerns of the story line, rather than about specific personal concerns. For example, if telling a story of divorce, the facilitator can encourage the creation of the fictional story. Issues of betrayal, hurt, and abandonment are treated as elements of the protagonist's struggle. Details will provide both interest and believability, but no one in the group must take personal ownership of the story. All participants can assist in creating a believable outcome for the story, which engages them in the creative process of problem solving. Youth can, in this fashion, become expert problem solvers, so long as they do not own the problem personally. This process engages the entire group, and in this way, much of the work is done prior to the actual dramatic enactment.

"In the narrative mode, meaning is not a destination. It is a process." (Riley 1999, 43) This fine distinction separates theatre from drama. Whereas the product is the most important part of any theatrical endeavor, the dramatic process is the most important element of drama. Facilitators may observe adolescents gently placing plaster bandages on one another's faces, youth struggling to portray their career goals with song titles for an original CD, or young adults preparing an artistic piece to share with an anonymous recipient. In each instance, the facilitator is invited to share a very special relationship that goes far beyond any polished theatrical performance. Chapters 5 and 6 talk more about the role of the adult facilitator in the drama therapy process. However, the facilitator must be prepared to join the adolescent in the drama of the journey, enjoying the journey itself. The meaning is the journey.

Measuring Success

How would one measure success with teens? The art therapist Shirley Riley states the goal of all those working in the expressive arts:

> Therapy that doesn't seem like therapy because it is artwork; communication that transcends ordinary words by imagery and through metaphor; and a relationship with an adult that is not experienced as controlling; is a description of success with teen clients. (Riley 1999, 65)

Drama meets all these criteria. Because drama is the most inclusive of all the fine arts, including music, art, writing, and movement, it engages teens in a variety of expressive forms. The joy of this experience lies in the total involvement of the person, the spontaneity of the moment, and the abandonment of personal defenses. The drama experience may assist in reaching any of these four goals (Emunah 1994):

1. expression and containment of emotion
2. development of an observant self
3. expansion of role repertoire
4. social interaction.

Out-of-control adolescents may need more assistance with the first goal. They may be unable to modulate the expression of their emotions, and certainly they have been unable to contain those emotions. For example, an angry youth may express only anger and may need assistance in learning how to express hurt, fear, or loneliness, the primary emotions that lie behind the anger. By casting the youth in roles that demand a variety of emotional expressions, the youth can learn to identify and express emotions more appropriately.

The adult facilitator assists with the process of containment by assuring that the acting space is safe and secure. To provide that security, there will probably be no touching, and certainly there will be no hitting or fighting. The space must be secure for anyone who enters it. The facilitator must teach the meaning of the word *freeze* in the first session or two. This term indicates that all action will come to a halt, and participants will freeze in position. The facilitator may also direct teens to move in slow motion. By doing so, they must slow down both the physical and the mental processes, providing another form of containment. Other commands such as *curtain* may be used to indicate when the action begins and ends. These simple commands provide containment of the dramatic episode. They put the facilitator in charge of safety and security and provide a great deal of behavioral control. However, youth are still free to explore their creative side and given considerable leeway with the language and story portrayed. The ultimate goal is to enable youth to provide their own containment, or internal control, so they may function independently of the group.

The Observant Self

No drama is complete without an audience, so teens will also learn to develop an "observant self." In so doing, they must see themselves more objectively and examine the effectiveness of their words and actions. In order to develop that observant self, participants must be willing to play a variety of roles. All too often, youth are happy to just be themselves and delighted that they can see the rest of the world as totally different.

Role Reversal

When they are asked to "reverse roles," they must assume the role of the other person in the scene. The facilitator will teach this command early in the session so that the enactors immediately know they must switch roles. When they reverse roles, each person assumes the body, posture, and voice of the other individual. Each enactor is then forced to see himself as portrayed by someone else. The facilitator will call for a role reversal when the enactor needs to see the situation in a new light, when the enactor asks a question that only he can answer, or when the enactor needs someone else to assist with expressing the emotions of the scene (Sternberg and Garcia 2000). The facilitator will need to demonstrate the use of this command so that group participants feel comfortable with this change.

Such warm-up exercises as mirroring also assist with this process. As mentioned earlier, this exercise asks participants to mirror the movements of their partner so intently that eventually each person is unaware of who begins the movement. The mirroring exercise forces teens out of their narcissistic selves to focus on the movements of another and to eventually synchronize those movements.

Expanding Roles

Expansion of role repertoire is one of the primary goals of adolescence. Providing opportunities for playing different characters in new and different situations gives youth the chance to explore the many roles that lie within them, thereby expanding the many opportunities available to them in their ordinary lives. Adolescents who have an exceptionally difficult time expressing themselves may sometimes need a "double." The double may be an adult or another youth in the group. When groups are new, it is probably better for the facilitator to become the double, to demonstrate the feelings associated with this role. This person assumes the same posture and movement of the enactor but says what the enactor is thinking or feeling. The enactor still controls the situation because the enactor may restate the words as her own if they feel right or reject them if they feel wrong. As group members develop more empathy, they should be encouraged to double for other participants.

Some enactors will feel much more comfortable in trying new forms of expression if someone assists them with this process. In new groups, where youth may feel uncomfortable the first time they try expanding their roles, the facilitator may serve as the television talk show host. The authors often do so, pretending to hold a microphone and asking questions of each enactor. The facilitators can be as playful and absurd as they choose since they are in charge of the enactment. Usually youth will respond appropriately since they are responding only to the facilitator's questions. They do not even realize that they are expanding their roles exponentially simply by answering questions. In this process, "Expression becomes associated with creativity rather

Doubling helps demonstrate the feelings associated with a role.

than with volatile acting out. Adolescents learn that they can be actors rather than reactors." (Emunah 1995, 158)

Social interaction occurs naturally with youth, but the interaction may or may not be appropriate. Interpersonal skills, role training, and communication skills may be facilitated through drama. Traditional forms of role-playing assist with this process. But, because persons are usually on their own to enact the role-play, the success or failure of the experience has largely been dependent upon the acting ability of the participants. When the facilitator assists with this process, the enactors are never alone on the stage. Facilitators who incorporate drama into their groups must feel comfortable being in the middle of the action. The facilitator is willing to engage himself in the process, making himself as vulnerable as any group member. The facilitator can double for persons who may not know what to say, can reverse roles when enactors get stuck, and can suggest a variety of other techniques to keep the action moving.

Let us assume that you have a group of adolescents who are dealing with the issue of peer pressure. You set up a scene after school on a Friday, where plans are being made for the weekend. Some students will be ready to party, some students will be reticent to participate, and some absolutely refuse. You make the scene as realistic as possible so that the enactors get a chance to practice a variety of responses to this situation. If they get stuck, the adult facilitator can double for them, suggesting both enticements to party as well as responses that might be given to the enticements. Remember that the scene does not have to end happily. The process of the drama is its own best work. In the closing segment of the session, discussion may center on similar situations, other responses, and the feelings connected with this scene.

The two extremes of expression and containment may be necessary aims for the same individual. The facilitator is always encouraging group members to seek aesthetic distance—to balance thought and feeling, reality and fantasy. Both under-distanced individuals (those too close to their emotions) and over-distanced individuals (those too far away from their emotions) have to seek a balance (Landy 1993b). Abstract roles assist under-distanced teens by forcing them to use their intellect. Reality-based roles help over-distanced teens by forcing them to deal more with their emotions. Masks and other projective roles serve well for those who merge too much with their characters. The use of such objects forces them into a more playful, fantasy role. In the process of the drama, feelings do not have to be overwhelming, and reflection does not become just intellectualizing. Meaning still lies in the creative process itself (Landy 1991).

REFERENCES

Cossa, M., S. S. Fleischmann Ember, L. Grover, and J. L. Hazelwood. 1996. *Acting Out: The Workbook*. New York: Accelerated Development.

Emunah, R. 1994. *Acting for Real*. New York: Brunner/Mzel Publishers.

———. 1995. " From Adolescent Trauma to Adolescent Drama: Group Therapy with Emotionally Disturbed Youth." In *Dramatherapy with Children and Adolescents*, edited by Sue Jennings. New York: Routledge.

Jennings, S. 1995. "Dramatherapy for Survival: Some Thoughts on

Transitions and Choices for Children and Adolescents." In *Dramatherapy with Children and Adolescents*, edited by Sue Jennings. New York: Routledge.

Jones, P. 1996. *Drama as Therapy: Theatre as Living*. New York: Routledge.

Landy, R. J. 1991. "The Dramatic Basis of Role Theory." *The Arts in Psychotherapy*. 18, 29–41.

———. 1993a. "The Child, the Dreamer, the Artist and the Fool: In Search of Understanding the Meaning of Expressive Therapy." *The Arts in Psychotherapy*. 20, 359–370.

———. 1993b. *Persona and Performance*. New York: The Guilford Press.

Riley, S. 1999. *Contemporary Art Therapy with Adolescents*. Philadelphia: Jessica Kingsley Publishers.

Sternberg, P., and A. Garcia. 2000. *Sociodrama: Who's in Your Shoes?* Second Edition. Westport, CT: Praeger.

4

THE ADOLESCENT DRAMA

As adolescents embark on their journey, they may find themselves lost, misdirected, or confused. A variety of helping professionals may be entrusted with the duty of assisting these young people. Teachers, mental health professionals, and youth workers are often called upon to assist with this process. Parents and other adults refer teens for assistance when they have broken legal or social codes, when they defy adults and other authority figures, and when they strike out on a path that may be either unfamiliar or uncharted territory.

The primary job of adolescence is that of discovering one's own identity. In that process, the adolescent must try on many roles before discovering the ones that fit most appropriately. Drama may assist in that process by providing a safe and secure environment in which the adolescent may practice roles with little serious consequence. With proper guidance and understanding of the process, helping professionals may employ a variety of drama techniques that adolescents will find helpful and meaningful.

If your classroom or psycho-educational group has lost its zest and creativity or you have tired of waiting for your teen groups to generate their own issues, you might try incorporating drama into those groups. You will undoubtedly see an increase in attendance, more creativity in the group, and an increased amount of involvement by all group members. Drama can become a fairly non-threatening way to engage youth in highly interactive games, artistic exploration of issues, and playful intellectual and emotional stimulation.

Drama is an active and interactive use of the group process that values the creativity of its participants. It aims to engage the participants in telling and creating stories to assist with their own personal growth. The facilitator might assist developmentally disabled adults in creating a video on dating issues, or the facilitator might encourage teens of divorced parents to engage in a playful tug-of-war between the parents. The technique of the process will vary, depending upon the facilitator, the aims of the group, and the group dynamics.

The Role of Role

No drama takes place without characters enacting a role. No role exists without the willingness of a participant to assume that role. Adolescents on the journey to adulthood assume a variety of roles in the process of self-discovery. Many roles will be discarded, cast aside like unnecessary garments along the roadside when they are torn, outgrown, or ill suited for the journey. Other roles will remain with the adolescent for an extended period of time because, like comfortable garments, they feel right, they feel acceptable, and they look good. Some of these roles will remain with adolescents as they progress into adulthood. Only after an extended period of role experimentation do adolescents become capable of deciding which roles fit best.

Drama provides a safe and secure environment in which the adolescent may experiment with these roles. The role connects everyday life, drama, and the experience of the group itself (Landy 1993). For example, you might have an overachiever in your group. This individual may be a stellar student, and she may provide for many of the physical and emotional needs of the family. If that same individual is cast as a clown in the circus or a mischievous youngster, another role may emerge. On the surface, the roles may appear quite dissimilar. But as the drama progresses, the new role is allowed to develop in whatever manner the person desires. Later, as the enactor reflects upon her emotional reaction to the role, new understandings of the self may emerge. The everyday role of the overachiever, the drama of the new role, and the benefit of the experience merge in the process of the dramatic enactment.

Name the Role

Drama casts individuals in a variety of roles. At one point the adolescent may be the actor; at another point the adolescent may be the director. At other times, youth may serve as audience, musician, or storyteller. As each new role is assumed, the role is named. Naming a role allows one to establish distance from that role, rather than being captured by the role (Emunah 1994). For example, the process of naming the overachiever, the mischievous child, and the clown gives an individual some control over those roles. Bringing these roles to consciousness and accepting their existence also allows one to reevaluate the role and change it. Linda recalls being told by a university writing instructor that if she wanted to hold on to her memories, she should not write about them. At first she was offended by that thought, preferring to hold on to frightening and debilitating memories, rather than run the risk of losing them. She now knows that the instructor meant that once she had committed the memory to paper, and even more importantly, once she had shared those memories publicly, the memories would lose some of their emotional power. The process of transforming memories into a poem, an essay, or a work of fiction put the memories in an objective realm that allowed them to be treated as a work of art, rather than a nightmare. Emunah (1994) speaks of this objectification as a form of detachment that is similar to that of certain spiritual traditions. In these traditions, meditation and other forms of disentanglement are practiced in order to help one move from imprisonment to freedom.

Experiment with Variety

As roles are expanded and youth experiment with more variety, they learn to see themselves both as themselves and not as themselves. Landy (1991) calls this taking of the role as the "not-me." The "not-me" role can be examined, questioned, or adapted as necessary, for the role does not threaten the individual. Of course, the facilitator is well aware that the individual reveals as much of himself when in role as when out of role. But, remembering that the dramatic process does its work, the facilitator will allow the enactors to come to this understanding at their own pace. Because drama is a brief experience, the youth are not committed to an in-depth commitment to their roles. The group experience becomes a safe laboratory where one can experiment with a variety of roles that can be quickly discarded or revised.

Youth may need to be reminded that their commitment to role is a short-term commitment, and they may need to be reminded that roles are simply "pretend" so they do not label one another. This advice is especially important for youth from dysfunctional families where youth may be frightened when engaging in new and unfamiliar roles. They may either highly restrict the roles they play or quickly assume a role without question (Emunah 1995). The facilitator may need to remind youth to shake off their roles when the enactment ends so that youth do not confuse "pretend" with "reality."

Be Aware of Ambivalence

Adults recognize that most roles are quite complex, and our relationship to those roles may be quite ambivalent. Individuals are not one-dimensional beings with easy explanations of motivations, dreams, hopes, or fears. If youth are unable to handle the ambivalence of a role, they will create roles with only one dimension (Landy 1993). For example, such a person might be unable to understand how a teenager could both love his parents and disagree with them at the same time. He might create a teenager who could only fight with his parents because they restrict his freedoms. When faced with such a dilemma, it is sometimes helpful to set up extremes at either side of the room. In this case, love and indifference might be the polar opposites. The facilitator can ask other participants to represent these opposites. Those persons can shout advice to the enactor, trying to draw him to their side. If the enactor remains stuck in one position, the volume and intensity of the other extreme can increase. As the enactor moves back and forth between the two extremes, he begins to recognize his own ambivalence.

On the other hand, youth with too much ambivalence suffer confusion when trying to master a role (Landy 1993). They may be unable to create dialogue and action that are meaningful because they are so uncertain about their own identity. Their struggles with role may almost paralyze them in the process. The use of doubling works well to assist such youth whose spontaneity is lost in the ambivalence. The individual in character may choose to use the line, thereby repeating it, or may choose to ignore the line. Doubling gives individuals the security of another person standing beside and assisting them through the gray areas of life and character. Of course, some role ambivalence is essential for the developmental process to proceed. The ability to see oneself and others as highly complex individuals is an important step in maturation. Recognizing ambivalence and the complexity of the individual's struggle does not mean an easy resolution to conflicts, but it may be the first step in transformation.

WARM-UPS FOR ADOLESCENT GROUPS

You might think of warm-ups as the stretching exercises that prepare us for the journey. Stretching warms our muscles, increases flexibility, and focuses our energy. Group warm-ups accomplish much the same purpose. As the classroom or group comes together for each session, they must get in touch with themselves and with other group members. These warm-up exercises serve to focus energy, increase spontaneity, and engage group members in the creative process. Sometimes facilitators forget that life experiences that take place in between class sessions or group meetings can have a profound effect upon group members. The warm-up serves as a way to get in touch with the group once again so that real work on true human issues can begin.

Some favorites are included here, beginning with those that are most appropriate for newly formed groups where group members may be totally unacquainted. The authors have used and adapted these warm-ups so many times that they have now become a part of their repertoire. But they wish to credit Viola Spolin for her work in *Improvisation for the Theater* for initially providing many warm-ups for use in improvisation. They also want to credit Patricia Sternberg and Antonina Garcia for the many fine warm-ups included in *Sociodrama: Who's in Your Shoes?* and give thanks to the excellent contributions of Sally Bailey's *Wings to Fly*.

Name Games
Name and Movement Game
Each person says her name and adds a movement appropriate to her name or her personality. For example, Wendy might blow as

if in the wind. Each person in the group then repeats the name and action of the person. Each group member then repeats her name and her action. The next time, as you go around the group, the group member repeats the name and action of the person to her left and then adds her own name and action. The third time around the participant begins by repeating her name and action. She then repeats the name and action of anyone else in the group. That person repeats her own name and action and proceeds with the name and action of someone else. Continue until all group members have been included.

Names and Rhythm

After group members are fairly well acquainted with each other's names, begin a rhythm such as hitting the knees twice, clapping twice and snapping fingers of the left hand and then fingers of the right hand. After the rhythm is established, the person who begins says his first name and then the first name of another group member as he snaps his fingers. The person whose name is called continues, repeating his own name and that of another group member. Continue until all are included and comfortable with the established rhythm.

Names and Objects Game

Place a variety of household objects in the center of the group. Ask each person to pick up an object that most closely resembles her. Each person then shares her name and explains how the object represents something about her.

Who's My Neighbor?

Participants will sit in chairs placed in a circle. Choose one person to come to the center of the circle, and remove his chair from the circle. That person may point to anyone in the group and ask, "Who's Your Neighbor?" The individual will respond, naming the first names of the persons to his left and right. Then he says, "I would like to meet everyone who has . . ." He must list something that is true about himself, such as "who has blue eyes" or "who brushed their teeth this morning" or "who has divorced parents." All persons who have that characteristic in common must change chairs, leaving one person in the middle of the circle.

Continue the action in this fashion until most persons have had the opportunity to be in the middle of the circle.

Warm-ups for New Groups

The Magic Box

Decorate an empty box. Each group member pretends to open the box and pantomimes actions to indicate what was found in the box. Other group members may join in the pantomime when they understand what is happening. Variation: Add an emotional response to this object and ask participants to show that emotion when opening the box.

Pass the Prop

Pass a simple prop around the group, such as a scarf or a black-board eraser. Each member pantomimes the use of an object about the same size and shape, showing how it would be used. Each person must use the prop in a different way, indicating its change into a different object. For example, the scarf might be a bandit's mask, a diaper, or a hula skirt.

Pass the Ball

Throw an imaginary ball around to group members. Each person must decide upon a size and weight before throwing the ball. The receiver will then change the size and weight before throwing the imaginary ball to another group member.

Statues

Divide group into units of three to four individuals. One person in each group is to be the sculptor. Give the group an emotion to sculpt (such as jealousy, pride, joy). The sculptor forms the body and facial expressions of each member in a manner that best exemplifies the emotion. Other group members must guess the emotion portrayed.

The Big Whopper

Divide the group into pairs. Each person is to get acquainted with her partner. The partners must not tell the truth to one another. However, their lies must in some way resemble the truth so that the lies are less obvious. After the initial discussion, partners will

Sculpting statues is a warm-up to dramatize emotions.

guess which parts of the story were the truth and which were lies. You can add to this activity by having each person introduce the partner to the whole group, telling three things about the partner. Let the group guess which statements were true and which were false.

The Talk Show

Divide group into pairs. Give the pairs five to ten minutes to get acquainted. They must find three interesting or unusual things about their partner. Then each will introduce his partner as a talk show host would do so, highlighting the interesting aspects of the guest.

The Line-up

Ask group members to line up by shoe size, by birth date, by height, by house numbers, or alphabetically by middle names. Use any other ideas you can think of. Allow the group to decide how to get organized. This warm-up serves as an excellent assessment of group leadership.

Advertising Yourself (Mahaffey 2001)

Bring in an assortment of art supplies: paper, markers, pastels, crayons, and so on. Ask each group member to prepare an advertisement or travel brochure for herself. As each person shares her artwork, she "sells" herself to the group.

Sentence Starters

Provide each participant with an envelope, art materials such as markers, paint, glitter, sequins, glue, and the sentence starters on white or colored paper. Type up these sentence starters and make a copy for each group member. Cut the sentence starters into strips and place in an envelope with each group member's name on the outside. Invite members to decorate the envelope. Allow the group members to select a sentence starter they would like to begin with. Members may use the art materials to express the ideas contained in the sentence starters, as well. Sample starters include the following:

> I feel I barely got through . . .
> Lately I've been . . .
> If I really thought about it, I'd . . .
> Every time I hear the word *Dad* I . . .
> Things would be better if I weren't so . . .
> No one would believe this but . . .
> One thing I like about myself is . . .
> When I was little I liked it when . . .
> It always feels so good when . . .
> I felt especially proud when . . .
> I fear I am inappropriate when I . . .
> My favorite treat is . . .
> I feel guilty when . . .
> Don't ever call me . . .
> I think it's so cute when . . .
> Don't even look at me when . . .
> I feel ashamed when I . . .
> My mother reminds me of a . . .
> When I see flowers I think of . . .
> Boy, I sure hate it when . . .
> I feel all out of control when . . .

I am scared of . . .
It's funny but . . .
I'll survive if . . .
I am really great at . . .
I feel silly when I . . .
I get so jealous when . . .
Usually I don't like to . . .

Putting It on the Line (Mahaffey 2001)

Ask students to design T-shirts to advertise themselves. You may ask them for specific items such as name, something they would like to share, or something of which they are proud. Or you may leave the directions open, allowing them to express whatever they desire. When students are finished, hang the T-shirts on the clothesline. When processing this experience, ask each student to stand by his shirt and explain whatever he would like to share with the group.

Warm-ups for Established Groups

Twenty-one

The goal of this warm-up game is for the group members to count to twenty-one, one person at a time, with no established order. Each person may say only one number. When any two persons say the same number at the same time, the group must start all over again. This exercise serves as a good assessment of the cohesion and sensitivity of the group.

Just What I Need

Pass around a small container, such as a wooden box. Explain that this object holds just what each participant needs at this moment. As each person receives the container, she states what emerges from the container. Another variation is to form an imaginary well with chairs, tables, or other props. Each person goes to the wishing well to draw from it exactly what she is in need of today.

Pass the Picture Frame (Hollander 1978)

Pass around an empty picture frame. Each person will imagine a picture for the frame. The picture will include the speaker. Each person explains what he sees as the frame is passed around the group.

Labeling

As participants enter the room, place a label (sticky note) on each person's forehead. The labels will include such phrases as these: doubt me, agree with me, respect me, make fun of me, ignore me, listen carefully to me, adore me, give me anything I want, treat me as a little child. No one is to tell the others exactly what the label says, but each participant will respond to the others according to the messages on their foreheads. Participants must then guess what the label says. This exercise is a good warm-up for issues involving stereotyping.

Linking the Silence

Make an open space in the middle of the room. Blindfold each group member or ask members to close their eyes. The group leader is the only person who is not blindfolded. Each person turns around two or three times and takes two steps forward. Each group member will try to locate the leader, who remains absolutely quiet. Group members wander around the room saying, "Hello." When a blindfolded person finds the leader, she removes the blindfold and joins the leader. All join hands to form a quiet group. Continue until everyone in the group becomes silent. This is an excellent warm-up for helping persons become aware of the quiet and easily ignored members of a group or organization.

Linking Body Parts

The leader calls out body parts like "elbow to elbow," and participants must touch that body part to another's. After two or three rounds, group members suggest such arrangements as "nose to hip," and so on.

Sculpting

Sculpt an object in the air and pass that object. The person who receives the object sculpts it into something else and passes it on. Continue until everyone has participated. Variations include sculpting emotions in pairs, sculpting self-portraits of the present

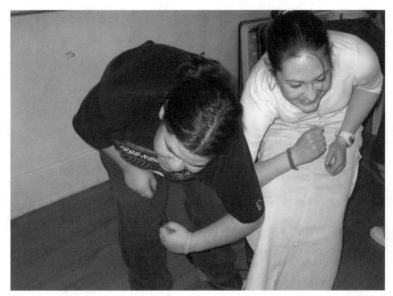

Linking Body Parts is a good warm-up for established groups.

and future, and sculpting inside and outside selves. Any of these can lead to more complete enactments.

Partner Pantomime

An individual decides upon an activity that he needs help completing. He pantomimes the activity. When another person catches on, he joins the pantomimed activity. Continue until all group members have participated.

Yarn Web

Use a ball of yarn to tell a story. As the story moves across the circle, the ball is passed from one to another, creating a web-like arrangement. Note the connections that group members make with one another through this exercise. Another variation occurs when the story is retold, passing the yarn back around the circle as the story is reworked and the web is untangled. For example, teens might tell a "family tradition story," making up events that occur during a holiday celebration. Encourage teens to make the story as realistic as possible, not necessarily a story with a moralistic ending. If the group would like to retell the story with a

Yarn Web warm-ups connect group members as they tell and retell a story.

different ending, encourage them to do so as they pass the string back around the circle and rework the story. This exercise may also be used as a closing exercise, noting the strength of the group's web when group members make a commitment to one another or to a group project. Linda has successfully used this exercise as a commitment exercise after teaching suicide prevention skills, where each participant makes a commitment about something she will do to help prevent teen suicide.

REFERENCES

Bailey, S. D. 1993. *Wings to Fly*. Rockville, MD: Woodbine House.

Emunah, R. 1994. *Acting for Real*. New York: Brunner/Mzel Publishers.

————. 1995. "From Adolescent Trauma to Adolescent Drama: Group Therapy with Emotionally Disturbed Youth. " In *Dramatherapy with Children and Adolescents*, edited by Sue Jennings. New York: Routledge.

Hollander, C. 1978. *The Warm-Up Box*. Denver: Colorado Psychodrama Center.

Landy, R. J. 1991. "The Dramatic Basis of Role Theory. " *The Arts in Psychotherapy*. 18, 29–41.

————. 1993. *Persona and Performance*. New York: The Guilford Press.

Mahaffey, J. 2001. Personal conversation.

Moreno, J. L. 1985. *Psychodrama* (Vol. 1). Fourth Edition. Ambler, PA: Beacon House.

Spolin, V. 1998. *Improvisation for the Theater*. Evanston, IL: Northwestern University Press.

Sternberg, P., and A. Garcia, 2000. *Sociodrama: Who's in Your Shoes?* Second Edition. Westport, CT: Praeger.

5

ROADBLOCKS, DETOURS, AND TRAFFIC CIRCLES

Once we embark on any journey, we know that we waste a lot of time with roadblocks and detours. However, if we are aware of the situation before it arises, it is easier to plan ahead and take an alternate route. Even if we take more time to reach our destination, we are better prepared for that alternative. In that same sense, we urge you to read this chapter before proceeding. Many of us are tempted to look ahead and see "how to do it" before considering "why we do it." Please read this chapter carefully before proceeding. It will assist you in setting up adolescent groups for more success. The "how to do it" sections will follow in Chapters 6–8.

SETTING UP A GROUP

Adolescent groups can be highly effective if they are planned and executed in a clear, creative, and forthright manner. Before organizing a group, consider the setting in which it will take place and the kind of group you will lead. The information here refers to school groups, prevention activities, and support groups.

Open-ended Versus Close-ended

Before setting up the group, consider whether it will be an open-ended group or a close-ended group. Open-ended groups accept membership at any time. Therefore, the group composition may change at every session. Close-ended groups start with the same persons and continue in that fashion until their termination. Close-ended groups often experience considerably more growth among members because they develop cohesion, trust, and caring in a depth that is not possible when the group membership changes frequently. School classrooms are normally close-ended groups, although you may see some fluctuation in membership. Open-ended groups continually force the group to deal with change. Some groups can handle that kind of constant movement, but others cannot.

Also consider how much homogeneity you wish in your group. You probably want enough homogeneity to develop cohesion in the group. However, too much homogeneity may create a stalemate. Some variety in membership will provide more interest and stimulation to the group (Malekoff 1997). Also beware that recent studies show negative outcomes result when high-risk youth are placed in the same peer group. They appear to reinforce the negative behaviors of each other (National Institute on Drug Abuse 2003). Of course, sometimes you have no control over the makeup of the group. The classroom teacher has little control over group membership. The school counselor, on the other hand, might be able to pick and choose members for a psycho-educational group. The techniques will still work if you make necessary adaptations based upon the group dynamics. You may wish to work with a group of adolescents whose parents have recently divorced, for instance. You will probably establish an age range that you find acceptable, and you will decide how many members you would like to have in the group. Usually a group of five to ten members works the best, but we have worked with both larger and smaller groups quite successfully. Your approaches just vary somewhat by the size and complexity of the group.

Determine Meeting Space

Next, determine the space in which your group will meet. Drama normally needs a bit larger space than might be used for a group meeting. You need a room large enough to allow movement of all participants but small enough to create some sense of cohesion. If your room is rather large and cavernous, create a smaller area within that room in which you will do your group work. You do not need a stage, and in fact, a stage may inhibit the process of the group because it makes teens feel as if they are truly engaged in a performance rather than a process. If possible, try to obtain a space that will allow action to take place either at one end of the room or in the center of the room. You can easily guide teens to imagine where the acting space exists.

Decide on Leadership

Decide from the outset whether you will lead this group alone or will engage the use of a co-leader. A co-leader can assist in looking for dynamics that the drama facilitator might miss while leading the process. A co-leader also can be invaluable if someone in the group gets upset and asks to leave the group. It is important that someone accompany the youth if this situation should arise. However, the involvement of a co-leader requires a commitment on the part of both leaders to plan and debrief each session together.

> One consequence of poorly conceived coworkership in adolescent groups is the fallout from unexpressed differences about the rules, structure, composition, content, or goals of the group. (Malekoff 1997, 66)

If you can locate a co-leader who is willing to commit the time to this work and is willing to work with you on establishing the structure and content of the group, take advantage of that commitment. If you cannot locate such a person, it is certainly possible for you to lead these drama activities by yourself.

ROLE OF THE FACILITATOR

The facilitator who uses drama in a group must be well organized and flexible. Malekoff calls this "planned emptiness," a willingness to provide structure while remaining open to the uncertainty and surprise provided by the group event itself (Malekoff 1997, 20). This leader is willing to learn from the group and is willing to change course according to the group's interest. The group facilitator must embrace the fluidity of the group and be willing to ride the current, even when it seems that whitewater lies ahead. Michael Rohd (1998, 3) compares this work to a journey in the following manner,

> The process is a journey. Like any journey, it has a beginning, a route, and a schedule, but it does not have a predetermined destination. It just gives direction to start. (Rohd 1998, 20)

Provide Structure

But the leader also has planned ahead and organized activities to meet the goals of the group. It is especially important to provide structure and predictability when working with youth from dysfunctional situations.

> Young people living in families that are seriously dysfunctional may be hypervigilant, endlessly surveying the scene for land mines. Structure, predictability, flexible handling, clarity, and consistency in the group over time, are all necessary precursors to developing a feeling of trust. (Malekoff 1997, 45)

As professional adults, we are often expected to change our plans at the last minute and adapt to new situations without warning. Always keep in mind that these teens need the safety of the structure that you may provide. Knowing when and where the group will meet and relying on the presence of the group facilitators are essential to them. Do not be distracted and convinced that the change of date and location are just minor inconveniences.

Define the Purpose

The content and purpose of the group must be consistent. The leaders must be clear about the purpose of the group, and they should discuss the purpose with the adolescents so they can articulate it as well. Leaders must carefully choose activities that are consistent with the purpose of the group. Those activities make up the content of the group. All too often, facilitators choose activities that they enjoy with little or no thought to the purpose behind the activity. Those activities may engage the youth quite effectively, but they will have little impact upon the goals and objectives of the group unless they are consistent with the group's purpose.

Plan and Organize Activities

Engaging in drama requires a commitment to plan activities and provide the necessary materials or equipment. Such advance planning allows the facilitator to react spontaneously. As paradoxical as it may seem, planning and flexibility must go hand in hand. Often, groups function with little advance planning, but they also suffer from lack of engagement and effectiveness. When

Linda first started working with adolescent groups, she made the mistake of following co-leaders who thought they could just wait for issues to emerge from the group. The groups met weekly with little or no growth or progress. The leaders failed to plan and organize activities and relied on the teens themselves to provide their own insight. Obviously, that was an ineffective way to run a group. Teens need the structure and organization provided by the group leader.

Issues regarding control always arise when discussing group dynamics. Undoubtedly you will have colleagues who see youth engaged in playful activities while in your group, and they may question whether any "real work" is being done. Keep in mind that "Work and play in young people's groups are inseparable" (Malekoff 1997,148). You will likely accomplish more with a playful sense of joy and a willingness to be foolish than you will with a deadly serious tone. It helps if the facilitator can remain in contact with the childlike wonder experienced in younger years. That sense will allow you to see that work and play are intimately connected in the minds and hearts of the young.

Those of us who work with adolescents realize that control is a tricky issue. If you appear overly controlling, you will create a battleground in which teens play out their frustrations with authority figures. On the other hand, if you lose all control, you will have nothing but chaos, and you will accomplish no one's goals. Drama demands an openness to the process, a willingness to look foolish at times, and a desire to provide the most creative outlet for expression. Of course, uncomfortable issues will surface, but if the facilitator backs away from those issues, teens will sense that desire to retreat. It usually occurs because the facilitator feels anxious about the issue. Remember that our goal for all teen groups is to allow them to function more appropriately when they gain their independence. Therefore, "the members' taking over control of the group is to be valued when complemented by the worker's letting go of control" (Malekoff 1997, 96).

Much of contemporary society sees "play" as a competitive activity. Witness the numerous outlets for soccer, baseball, football, and so on. The facilitator must remember that the playful activities selected for groups should normally not be competitive.

Of course, occasionally one might use a team race or similar activity to engage in team building. But these teens are constantly involved in competition. There should be no "winners" or "losers" in your group. There are fine noncompetitive sports and games that can build group cohesion. See Terry Orlick's books on cooperative sports and games for excellent suggestions.

GROUP DEVELOPMENT

Since teens are normally very much influenced by their peers, they seek interaction with others on a continual basis. As a result of these interactions, they develop their own relational style. The adult facilitator may not be able to comprehend the full meaning of that style or the latest slang that accompanies it. However, the facilitator must be willing to allow the teen's culture to emerge. The facilitator must try to join that culture, not to change it. Of course, the adult will look silly and inappropriate if he tries to become a part of the culture. Nevertheless, he must learn to respect it and understand it as much as possible, keeping in mind the criteria for appropriate behavior (Malekoff 1997).

Those who feel uncomfortable with teens will often scoff at those of us who work with them, wondering if we need a frontal lobotomy before we proceed on this journey with them. The characteristic that most frightens adults is teen rebelliousness. Keep in mind the many intellectual, emotional, physical, and spiritual changes that youth experience. Some of the rebellion is simply a reaction against the increasing demands and responsibilities of approaching adulthood. While they look forward to the many freedoms of adulthood, they crave the protection of childhood (Emunah 1985). Many of you have probably noticed the remarkable change in behavior that occurs once a teen reaches the age of eighteen. Since they can then be treated as an adult, some demand those freedoms. On the other hand, the consequences for illegal activity escalate dramatically, and some will suddenly get a change of heart when faced with jail or prison time.

Renee Emunah (1985) has done the best job of outlining the issues of adolescent resistance and drama. We refer to her work throughout this section, adding our own experiences as valida-tion of her work.

Since rebellious acting-out is a normal developmental process, the facilitator may use that rebellion in the dramatic enactments. After all, teen enactments that do not portray adolescent rebel-lion are probably not very realistic. On the other hand, resistance occurs when persons become aware of unconscious issues and experience the uncomfortable feelings connected with those issues. Teens may use rebellion as a way to conceal those feelings. The facilitator sometimes may join the teen in rebellious behav-ior in order to engage the youth, and in doing so, the facilitator will bypass the resistance (Emunah 1985). If participants engage in truly rebellious behavior, the facilitator may ask them to exag-gerate that behavior to see if they can truly stay in character and remain as rebellious as they desire.

Development Phases

Groups normally go through several phases of development. There are usually three or four phases of group development if the group continues to meet over an extended period of time. We refer to these phases as Beginning, Middle, and End. Keep in mind that each phase of group development may last for several sessions, or it might be limited to only one session. Each group will vary, and some groups will not progress through all three phases.

Beginning Phase

The most challenging of all phases is the Beginning Phase. During this time teens are uncertain about group expectations and even more uncertain about themselves. During the first ses-sion the facilitator must engage the group in setting its purpose in words that can be clearly understood by all group members. Teachers normally establish those goals during the first week. Other facilitators may need to become more intentional in estab-lishing such guidelines. For example, teens from divorced families might establish "the improvement of communication with par-ents" as one of their group goals. If group members start to engage in blaming behaviors when talking about parents or enacting conflict resolution scenes around family issues, they may need to be reminded of the communication skills goal. Engaging in the use of "I statements," for example, would be a way of improving communication. When the purpose of the group is clearly understood by all members, the facilitator can remind the group of the goals if they should begin to stray from their purpose.

Group norms must also be established in the first session. Confidentiality must clearly be stated as one of the rules. When working with school and prevention groups, it is essential that group members know that "what is said in group stays in group" unless persons are in danger to themselves or others. Of course, if you use these techniques in a classroom setting, confidentiality is probably not an issue. But in that situation you will want teens to respect and trust other class members. Many of these techniques can be used effectively to teach life skills. Other rules should come from the group members. You may want to deal with issues of tardiness, listening, and other behavioral concerns.

We suggest that all groups follow three guidelines, presented at the Beginning Phase: Respect, Connect, and Participate. If teens respect one another, they will be considerate of one another's feelings, be supportive of one another, be tolerant of other's opinions, and be aware of boundaries. When they connect with each other, they will listen, take turns, work toward conflict resolution, and discover ways in which they are similar to each other. When they participate, they will actively engage in activities. However, they do reserve the right to pass on activities that might be too threatening. You will need to decide how you handle the issue of failure to participate. All group members have the right to pass, but if they should fail to participate on a repeated basis, they should probably visit with the facilitator about the situation. The four R's of any group, again, presented at the Beginning Phase, include these: (1) Respect for self, (2) Respect for others, (3) Responsibility for own actions, and (4) Right to pass.

During this Beginning Phase you will likely see some resistance to drama activities. The resistance is usually due to one or more of these factors:

1. performance anxiety
2. fear of looking childish
3. fear of acting like someone else (Emunah 1985).

Performance anxiety is a common issue. Youth who are self-conscious feel even more so if they feel as if they are "on stage" the minute they come to group. Beginning activities should allow teens to remain in their chairs so they feel more comfortable. You can use most of the activities suggested in the warm-ups in Chapter 4 during this phase. In fact, you should not progress beyond the warm-up phase for the first several sessions, just so teens begin to feel comfortable with themselves and one another. Some groups will never progress past the warm-up stage. You, as a group facilitator, may determine if the group is ready to move beyond this stage. Some teens refer to this part as the "playing games" stage.

Remember that teens want to be treated like adults, even though they crave the advantages of their childhood. They definitely do not want to look childish. For that reason, you need to choose your drama activities wisely. Avoid activities such as childhood games, puppets, and children's stories. Some of these activities work exceptionally well with younger children and with adults, but adolescents will be completely turned off if they think you are treating them like children.

Teens are often pretty insecure in their identity. For this reason, taking on the role of someone else is rather frightening. In the beginning, let them be themselves. You can gradually encourage them to take on new roles, but to do so at the very beginning is to invite disaster. A favorite Beginning Phase activity is the Talk Show. (See Warm-ups for New Groups in Chapter 4, pages 52–55.) If used in the first one or two sessions, the facilitator probably needs to serve as the Talk Show host. As mentioned earlier, the facilitator can engage in the enactment and model appropriate behavior for the group. Just pretend to hold a microphone in front of each group member and ask questions on the behalf of the listening audience. Encourage audience participation by asking the other group members what they would like to know. If inappropriate questions are asked, the facilitator can monitor them without exposing group members to embarrassment.

You are likely to find more resistance to involvement in the Beginning Phase than in any other phase of group development.

For this reason, the facilitator needs to feel confident that the activities are appropriately chosen to meet the purposes of the group and be assured that the group process will work. As Pat Sternberg always tells her students, "Trust the work" (Sternberg 1999). If you feel confident, teens will follow your lead and begin to trust the work you do together.

If teens offer resistance, they usually are trying to engage the facilitator in a power struggle. Remember that struggle with authority figures is a natural part of their development. However, if the facilitator refuses to struggle, there is no power struggle. Here are some suggestions for dealing with such resistance. If a youth appears hostile or aggressive, try to incorporate that feeling into an exercise. Renee Emunah (1985) gives a great example of a teen who refuses to get out of his chair. The facilitator challenges the youth to see how long he can stay in the chair. The teen must work just as hard to stay in the chair as the facilitator works in trying to get him out of the chair, gently pulling on him. Such an activity activates the resistance, rather than suppressing it, but it does so in a playful manner.

Some youth may feel so uncomfortable that they want to leave the group. You might engage the group in guessing games that allow one person at a time to leave the group. A favorite activity involves the establishment of a specific place (such as a tennis match, bus stop, or movie theatre). The remaining members of the group must pantomime activities that would take place in that scene. When the person who has left the room returns, she must guess the setting. This activity builds group cohesion while still allowing one person at a time to exit the situation and still remain engaged in the activity.

If the group members appear to be getting out of control, try to establish a scene in which there is a great deal of control. Linda recalls the day her group enacted a court scene. They knew far more about juvenile court than she did, and they thoroughly enjoyed taking on the roles of lawyer and judge. Sometimes youth also feel rather hopeless. If so, give them the right to establish an imaginary place that exceeds their present expectations. This activity can begin with an art activity where teens are asked to draw their ideal space. That way they do not have to begin by talking about the issue. Then you can encourage them to write about that place before talking about it.

It is often helpful to begin groups with pantomime and sculpting activities. Since students do not have to talk in these activities, they will begin to feel more comfortable with dramatic activities. The first drama concept to teach is "freeze." When the facilitator gives this command, all persons in the enactment must freeze into position immediately. This command accomplishes several things. First of all, the facilitator can control the action and stop anything that might result in violence or inappropriate touching. Secondly, it allows youth to examine the nonverbal dynamics of the scene. They can step out of the scene one at a time and see what it looks like. A Beginning Phase sculpting activity involves work in pairs or small groups of three or four youth. Give each group a feeling to sculpt, such as fear, joy, sadness, anxiety. (See Chapter 4 warm-up on Statues, page 52.) Ask one person to serve as sculptor. That person will move the other person(s) into a position that will reveal the feeling. Other group members must guess the feeling. This helps groups become more conscious of nonverbal expressions of feelings and allows touching to take place in an appropriate manner. If you work with a co-leader, the two of you can demonstrate this activity before beginning.

Consider for a moment what happens in the normal development of a child. After the child leaves the Terrible Twos, the first stage of rebellion, he enters the stage of dramatic play. At this time, anyone and anything can become something else. Preschoolers play house, cops and robbers, and doctor during this stage. During the Beginning Phase, the facilitator will gradually move the group into the stage of dramatic play. The dramatic play gives the child control over a fantasy world, even though he has no control over the real world. In the same way, adolescents can begin to gain control of their own destiny. "Dramatic play provides the distance necessary for the self-observing ego and thus a sense of self-mastery and internal control." (Emunah 1985, 75)

Middle Phase

When the group moves into the Middle Phase, real enactments may begin. The enactments are likely to be more spontaneous, and teens will likely have overcome their fear of being seen. However, because of the permissiveness allowed in the Beginning Phase, teens are likely to act out the destructive patterns of their own life. In doing so, they can participate in the group activity but still look "cool." Emunah (1985) emphasizes how important it is for facilitators to accept the teen's choice of material. If facilitators censor subject material at this point, they are likely to meet immediate resistance. The facilitator must encourage adolescents to act out their own scenes. However, the facilitator will direct the scene. Doing so allows the facilitator to begin interventions. Several years ago Linda led a group in the Dragon activity described in Chapter 7. After some discussion about the role of a dragon in a story, each teen prepared a clay dragon and then painted it. Group members then explained their personal dragons. As the enactment played out, the group was enacting a Slayer concert, with the dragon figure on the stage. The facilitator's immediate reaction was one of total dread, for in spite of her attempts to move them beyond Slayer, they had once again returned to familiar territory. But Pat Sternberg's words, "Trust the work," kept playing in the back of her mind. She asked the group how they might begin to tame the dragon. And lo and behold, the concert audience embraced the dragon with love and care until the dragon's fear and anger dissipated. In this instance the facilitator accepted the material of the group but led the intervention.

Of course, the group may not always end the scene with a happy or appropriate conclusion. Linda remembers working with a group of freshmen, dealing with goal setting. Their goal was to get a high school diploma. (See A Game Plan in Chapter 7, page 96 for details.) They set up an imaginary playing field in the front of the classroom. The diploma was at one end. Students suggested a variety of obstacles that might prevent graduation. Then they chose a protagonist to try to work her way through the obstacles. Class members suggested ways the protagonist might overcome each obstacle, but some were insurmountable. The issue of health finally stymied the protagonist so that she did not reach her goal. This situation promoted discussion about how to tackle obstacles that many of them might face in the next four years. There may still be resistance in the Middle Phase, but if the facilitator accepts the material, teens will gradually accept the direction of the facilitator.

End Phase

When youth move into the End Phase, they usually will accept interventions without resistance. Keep in mind that not all groups will progress to this point, but if they continue to meet over time, the facilitator can begin to see real work going on. The facilitator may move the enactment beyond the realistic portrayal of a teen's present experience to either the past or future. In doing so, the teen can establish distance between himself and the role he is asked to play. For example, in the Back to the Future exercise explained in Chapter 7, pages 98–99, teens are asked to project ten years into the future and make a phone call back to themselves today. They explain where they are, what they are doing, and give advice to the teen of today. This exercise gives the teen distance between his real self and the self of the future. Teens may show an amazing amount of insight when allowed to change the time of an event. It is much less threatening to give advice from the future than to give it from the present. Similarly, youth can be asked to create the past that might explain present events, such as the events that led up to an encounter with the police, a fight with the parents, or a bad party scene.

During the End Phase, youth should also be encouraged to try on a variety of roles. Doing so expands their perspective and allows them to develop empathy with others. It is especially important that they have the experience of playing authority roles since they are in such conflict with authority figures at this point in their lives. The facilitator may wish to use the "freeze" technique at this point so that the teen can be taken out of the scene to observe the nonverbal communication. Freezing the scene may be used as a way to get perspective for the entire audience and a way to seek alternative solutions to the problem enacted. Of course, students learn a great deal from playing themselves, but they can also benefit from playing the roles of others (Emunah 1985).

In general, teens prefer to play realistic scenes, rather than fantasy scenes. This gives them more of an adult perspective and will not seem so childish. However, over time it is possible to add some fantasy to their experiences.

As teen groups prepare for the end of their time together, they must be given the opportunity to explore their feelings of closure and loss. As they prepare for their separation, be prepared for some of the following behaviors to occur (Malekoff 1997):

1. reawakened dependency needs
2. exclusion of the facilitator
3. regressive behavior
4. devaluation of the experience
5. flight.

Youth may not have learned how to make closure appropriately, and rather than face their own feelings, they may act inappropriately. Those who feel fearful about leaving the group may express extreme dependency, relying on the group and the facilitator more than necessary. Because youth wish to see themselves as independent, they may begin to exclude the facilitator in order to convince themselves that they no longer need adult assistance. Regressive behavior, which may appear somewhat childish, occurs so that the facilitator will once again direct attention to the individuals in the group. If youth devalue the importance of the group, saying, "This has been a waste of time," they usually are simply unable to express the actual dependency needs that have been addressed during the group experience. Flight patterns are some of the most difficult to deal with because teens will simply exit the group and refuse to attend as the group nears its termination. These teens may always have avoided good-byes and farewells and feel uncomfortable dealing with their feelings of loss.

It is essential to deal with the separation issues that will arise when the group nears its termination. The facilitator should address termination issues in a timely manner, giving teens time to address their feelings. But do not address this issue too early in the group's development. A great termination exercise is the Mail Box. Teens are asked to write a note to each person in the group and place those notes in the appropriate teen's box (or shoe or paper bag or something similar). Teens need not share their notes aloud, but they can take these very personal messages with

Hot Seat is a powerful closure activity that leaves each group member with an array of compliments.

them when they leave the group. There are many variations on this activity. Another is the Hot Seat, where teens, one at a time, sit in the middle of the circle. The group members give the teen compliments, and the teen in the center is only allowed to say, "Thank you." This is an especially powerful activity. The facilitator must be willing to sit in the middle, as well. Remember that facilitators should never ask teens to do something that they are unwilling to do themselves.

What is a roadblock? What is a detour? What is a traffic circle? Sometimes they will look like each other. What may be a roadblock at one session may prove to be only a detour at the next session. And what look likes a traffic circle, with several possible exits, may be a roadblock. But the facilitator who remains open to the process, trusting of the group, and spontaneous in her reactions will reap the rewards of the journey.

REFERENCES

Emunah, R. 1985. "Drama Therapy and Adolescent Resistance." *The Arts in Psychotherapy*. 12, 71–79.

Malekoff, A. 1997. *Group Work with Adolescents*. New York: The Guilford Press.

National Institute on Drug Abuse. 2003. *Preventing Drug Use Among Children and Adolescents*. Second Edition. Bethesda, MD: U.S. Department of Health and Human Services.

Orlick, T. 1978. *The Cooperative Sports and Games Book*. New York: Pantheon Books.

———. 1982. *The Second Cooperative Sports and Games Book*. New York: Pantheon Books.

Rohd, M. 1998. *Theatre for Community, Conflict & Dialogue*. Portsmouth, NH: Heinemann.

Sternberg, P. 1999. Personal conversation.

Yalom, I. D. 1983. *Inpatient Group Psychotherapy*. New York: Basic Books, Inc.

6

CREATIVE SIDE-TRIPS

Adolescents love to express themselves. Adolescents also love variety. Using too much of one technique becomes boring. An important role of the helping professional working with adolescents is finding creative avenues to structure and foster their expressions. Integrating each of the creative arts—drama, poetry, art, music, dance/movement—into the work you do with adolescents will improve attention, increase participation, and open engagement. Ultimately these experiences will lead to an increase in self-esteem and self-image, and appropriate, healthy social interactions. School, friends, parents, feeling different, anger, feeling dumb, not meeting expectations of themselves as well as of their parents, the body and sexuality—these are just a few of the issues that concern adolescents (Oaklander 1988). Pair the right creative art or arts with the right issue and you will have a match that will yield a super outlet for expression for the adolescents with whom you work.

PACKING FOR EVERYONE

Multiple Intelligences and the Arts

Howard Gardner's theory of multiple intelligences suggests that there are many ways of being smart. Incorporating more than one creative art into activities with adolescents can also accommodate individual learning styles and types of intelligences. Gardner categorizes the multiple intelligences into eight areas (Gardner 1985):

verbal-linguistic
math-logic
spatial

bodily-kinesthetic
musical
interpersonal
intrapersonal
naturalistic.

Adolescents with verbal-linguistic intelligence learn best through reading, speaking, writing, and discussing. This intelligence lends itself well to drama activities such as poetry, scripts, and improvisational dialogues as well as to art activities that include a gestalt dialogue for images. Those with mathematical-logic intelligence learn best through working with patterns and relationships or working with the abstract. Creative arts activities that enhance this intelligence include ones that involve deductive and inductive reasoning, sequencing, patterning, and pattern recognition. Spatial intelligence is best stimulated by activities that include working with pictures and colors, visualizing, using the mind's eye, and drawing. Adolescents with this intelligence love art activities. Bodily-kinesthetic intelligence is extremely suited to creative arts activities since adolescents with this intelligence learn best through touching, moving, and processing knowledge through bodily sensations. Drama games, dance/movement activities, pantomime, sculpting, drawing, painting, photography, and collage work stimulate and enhance this intelligence. Musical intelligence is best expressed through singing and creating rhythms. Adding rhythm to share feelings in an activity is a great way to allow adolescents with this intelligence to express themselves. Adolescents with interpersonal intelligence will love group work since their strength lies in understanding people, leading, organizing, communicating, resolving conflicts, and cooperating. Those with intrapersonal intelligence prefer activities where they can work alone, do self-paced projects, and have time to reflect. Naturalistic intelligence is best suited to adolescents who love working in nature and exploring living things. Activities that include nature objects or doing activities outdoors stimulates adolescents with this intelligence (Nicholson-Nelson 1998; Bailey 1997).

There are different ways to pair creative arts activities with multiple intelligences. You will have to discover what method works best for you by experimenting to see what works and what doesn't. Know that every group is unique and what is successful with one group may not be successful with another group. Sometimes that just means tweaking aspects of an activity to address the uniqueness of each group.

THREE IMPORTANT FACTORS FOR SUCCESSFUL CREATIVE SIDE TRIPS

Know Yourself

Before getting started, there are some basic factors leaders should know. First of all, you must know yourself (Warren 1993). Ask yourself:

> What are your strengths in terms of using the creative arts?
> Which creative art interests you most?
> Which do you find the most difficult to use?
> Which creative arts would you like to know more about or gain more confidence in using?
> How does using the creative arts make you feel?
> Are you comfortable with drama, art, music, dance/movement, or poetry?
> Which creative arts would you feel comfortable using only with individuals?
> Which would you feel comfortable using in groups?

A successful leader is one who is aware of his strengths and areas that need honing. Adolescents quickly find a leader's vulnerabilities and can use that knowledge to destroy the group process, diminishing the authority and reputation of the leader. Thus, knowledge of self and security in that knowledge can help facilitate the controlled release of a group's creative energies. Group members have to trust the leader before trusting themselves, for it is the leader who ultimately sets the tone and direction for the session. A leader who knows his strengths and weaknesses and is able to admit them will be able to create an atmosphere of safety and security.

Know Varied Art Techniques

It is not only vital to have an understanding of your own working style and the medium of your choice but it is also important to have knowledge of different techniques within a particular medium in order to tailor activities compatible to the group's needs and abilities (Warren 1993). For example, if a leader's medium is art, she must be aware of the different types of techniques for creating art and whether or not the group can safely and easily use the tools needed for a specific art technique. In contrast, if a leader's medium is not art but the group's energy calls for that medium, then the leader must decide if and how she can incorporate that medium into the group activities. It will require learning about specific art techniques and practicing them outside of group to gain understanding of all that is involved. Experiment with the activity and gain firsthand knowledge about the necessary materials, the length of time required for the activity, the cleanup process, and the number of sessions required for the project. There is nothing worse than trying to force adolescents to complete an activity in one session that should have been stretched out over two or more sessions. And the opposite also holds true: it's best not to stretch out over two or more sessions something that could have easily been done in one. In addition, there are practical issues to consider, such as space, room setup, or access to water and electricity. Does someone else also use the space? Will it be safe to leave materials sitting around? Can you make noise, move around, or play music? Are others able to view the activity through windows or is the space private?

Know Your Group

Since individuals have varying needs and methods of creative expression, it is important for the leader to know the individuals within the group, in order to be aware of group process, group flow, and how each individual member fits into the group (Warren 1993). Consider:

What interests do individuals have?
Will you need magazines with pictures of cars, animals, people, musicians, or food for collage work?
Which creative art will truly match with whom?
Can individuals maintain focus for projects that take longer than one session?

Is the individual or group member ready for the activity that you plan?

This last question should be considered in terms of cognitive processing ability, social-emotional development, or psychological safety (for example, using sharps, such as scissors, sharp knives, or razor blades).

PLANNING FOR THE BUMPS IN THE ROAD

Working with adolescents and their quirks ensures that there will be bumps in the road, no matter which creative side trip you choose to take them on. So, an important word of advice: If an individual or group does not respond positively to a specific medium or creative art, try another one. Don't force it. It is often possible to return to the "rejected" medium in later sessions. Adolescents will be up-front and honest about whether or not they like a particular creative arts approach. Listen to them or you will lose them. However, just because they don't like something doesn't mean they can't at least try it. Just be careful in how you attempt to get them to give it a try. Usually it is best to come at them from a different angle and then add in the "rejected" medium in a way that is non-threatening, enjoyable, and helpful. Sometimes, though, it is just counterproductive to incorporate the "rejected" medium at all.

And a word of warning: Don't try to integrate different creative arts into an activity just because they sound good. Make sure that what you are asking adolescents to do has logical flow and compatibility. Some activities are more amenable to incorporating extensions using creative arts than others. With some art activities, for example, turning a part of it into a dramatic scene or adding a rhythm that expresses the adolescent's feelings associated with the art piece would be appropriate. Ask yourself, what is my purpose for incorporating more than one creative art into a particular activity? The old adage, "If the shoe fits, wear it; but if it doesn't fit, don't force it," is very true when it comes to putting activities together for adolescents.

CREATIVE SIDE TRIP SUGGESTIONS

Here are some sample exercises that incorporate more than one of the creative arts. Of course, feel free to adapt them to your specific style and group needs. Use the activities to formulate your own unique repertoire of exercises. Remember that different activities serve to warm up the group, engage the members in action, and bring closure for the group. Remember to de-role so that teens do not remain in their fictional roles.

Nameshare

(Finneran 2000)

Materials

White Paper
Markers, crayons, colored pencils, oil pastels, art sticks, and so on
Glitter glue or colored three-dimensional glues

Purpose of the Activity

The purpose of this activity is to help the group members develop boundaries around what is and is not appropriate to share early in the group process. It also is a safe way to introduce oneself to a group. Serves as a great warm-up.

Multiple Intelligences

Verbal-linguistic
Math-logic
Spatial
Bodily-kinesthetic
Interpersonal
Intrapersonal

Directions

Ask youth to use the letters of their name to create a way of sharing aspects of themselves that they want the group to know, such as their favorite color, type of music, hobby, pets, and so on. Ask them to think about the letters of their name and how each one can be incorporated into a visual example of who they are. They should remember that they are in total control of what they do and do not choose to share about themselves. When everyone is finished, they will be asked to share their name picture with the group, describing and explaining how the letters of their name represent them.

As leader, make your own nameshare ahead of time to share with the group. Doing this serves three purposes. First, it allows you to see all that is involved in the process (the use of the materials, the feelings associated with one's name, identifying what to share and what not share with others, and amount of time the activity would take for your group members to complete). Second, it provides the group a concrete example of the finished product and sparks questions about what variations can be employed. Third, the leader is able to model expectations for the group, establishing boundaries of what is appropriate to share with the group and how to share that information.

This is a basic art activity. However, other creative arts can be incorporated into the activity by including some extensions or adaptations. For example, the group might decide to create a scene at the playground where one member likes to play. Some members might want to create a poem using the letters of their name, like an acrostic poem.

My Calming Place

(Finneran 2000)

Materials

Shoe boxes of various sizes

"Found items" / items of importance to group members

Teens can gather items from home or on a walk, and so on. These items need to be collected by the teens so that there is special significance attached to what is placed in the Calming Place box.

Magazines or other items from which pictures and/or words can be cut

Glue / glue gun

Scissors

Miscellaneous items for decorating the boxes, such as yarn, string, glitter

Purpose of the Activity

The purpose of this activity is to help youth solidify their "calming place" in concrete form. This place would be a place where the teen feels calm and safe. It is a place where he would go to relax and be worry free. It is to be a self-soothing place where he can de-escalate angry feelings. It may be a place that provides inspiration during times of depression or hopelessness. It may be a place that provides escape from overwhelming pain. The calming place needs to be created by the teen so that the power of the box has come from within.

Multiple Intelligences

All

Warm-up

Do this warm-up at least a day ahead of activity so that teens can collect items for the box.

Have youth visualize a place in their minds where they feel totally safe and relaxed; a place where they feel calm; a place where they would go to calm down if things in life were hectic, overwhelming, frightening. Let them know that you plan to have them create a representation of that place in the form of a diorama: a three-dimensional box. It is helpful if you have created your own or have examples of dioramas so that youth understand what is expected. Ask them to think about the sounds, textures, objects, individuals, odors/scents, tastes, or movements in their calming place. There are many excellent relaxation scripts available. Select ones appropriate to the population with which you are working.

Directions

Have group members each choose a box. Spread out magazines and ask them to begin cutting out pictures or words that are representative of their calming place. They should then begin to arrange the items they have collected and the pictures they have

Lanell's calming place, representing a space where she feels safe and relaxed.

cut out and place them in their boxes until it feels right to them. Once they have the box arranged like they want, they can begin to glue the items and pictures in place. Even the outside of the boxes can be covered with pictures or other materials. It is important to decorate the lid, as well. The lid contains and protects the calming place and may serve as a stand for the box when open.

If done as a group activity, teens may choose to share their boxes and describe in detail their calming places. Let them know that this box can be kept in their rooms at home, some place where they can use it as a point of relaxation when things are getting to be too much.

As a dramatic extension of this activity, you might have teens create three-dimensional calming places using group members to represent various parts of their calming place. Sounds, smells, music, and so on could be added. This information may need to be shared a session ahead so that materials could be collected. Also, individuals could create the internal rhythm that they experience when visiting their calming place.

Instruments of Expression

(Finneran 2000)

Materials

Materials needed will vary by instrument.

Purpose of the Activity

The purpose of this activity is to allow teens to make instruments that they can then use to musically enhance other projects or simply play for fun.

Multiple Intelligences

Math-logic
Spatial
Bodily-kinesthetic
Musical
Interpersonal
Intrapersonal

Directions

Specific directions are provided for each instrument.

Rain sticks

Materials

> Laminating film tubes or tubes that are about 1/8" thick and 1" to 2" in diameter
> Newspaper (cut in 1" strips)
> Papier-mache mixture (basic one is just a mixture of flour and water)
> Acrylic paints, markers, stencils
> Nails (long enough to stick part way across the inside of the tube)
> Hammers
> Rice-popcorn-lentils mixture
> Duct tape

Directions

Hammer nails into the tube at various points. Try to create a web effect with the points of the nails so that the rice mixture will flow through the nails yet touch them, creating the sound of rain. Once the nails are pounded in, put duct tape on one end of the tube. Pour in some rice mixture and test the sound made as you turn the tube over. If not satisfied with the sound, add more nails or more rice mixture. When satisfied with the sound, duct tape the open end closed to seal the contents of the tube. Put papier-mache on the entire tube with at least two coats. Let dry between coats. When the papier-mache is done, paint with color of choice in various designs or styles. Enjoy!

Drums

Materials

   Gallon coffee (or other type) cans, tubes that are 8" or larger
      in diameter
   Clear, sturdy film to make cover for drum
   Duct tape
   Paints suitable to the can or tube used or papier-mache
   Optional: feathers, beads, or other embellishments to string
      and attach to drum for enhanced rhythm effect

Directions

Secure film to top of drum. Make sure it is stretched tightly across the top of the can or tube. Use duct tape to secure it. You may then paint or papier-mache the drum, using your own personal designs. Adding other items to enhance the rhythm effect is fun.

Rhythm Shakers

Materials

   Dried gourds (various shapes and sizes)
   Paints

Directions

Gourds can be found in stores in the fall. Store them in a dry area that is well ventilated. Turn them often to avoid molding. Once the gourds are light in weight, tap them sharply into the palm of the hand to loosen the seeds inside. Remember, these are fragile so don't hit them too hard. Paint if desired or leave natural.

Rhythm Sticks

Materials

Newspaper
Dowel rods, about 12" in length
Tape
Brown paper, grocery sack paper, or other colored paper
Clear contact paper
Acrylic paints

Directions

Roll newspaper tightly around the dowel rod and tape securely. Wrap tightly with brown/colored paper and glue along the seam. Paint designs onto the brown/colored paper. Take the contact paper and tightly roll around the stick to seal it. The ends may be taped to seal them. Use these personalized rhythm sticks to create rhythms of various sorts.

Courage Party

(Finneran 2000)

Materials

Poster paper
Hand stencil
Markers, crayons, paints
Glitter glue, sequins, construction paper shapes
Scissors

Purpose of the Activity

The purpose of this activity is to help individuals face termination from the group or to face a particularly difficult issue. It also offers individuals an opportunity to "give" something to another. This is a good closure activity for a group that has been together for a while. Members can make a *khamsa* (Gomez 1992)—a symbol of good luck—for all the other group members as a good-bye/good-luck ritual. Have snacks and drinks available if possible to make the courage party a true celebration.

Multiple Intelligences

This activity incorporates all except musical and naturalistic, depending on how the activity is done.

Directions

A *khamsa* is a good-luck symbol shaped like a five-fingered hand. It is a common symbol found in cultures of northern Africa and Mediterranean countries (Gomez 1992). Tell group members that they are to create a *khamsa* for the person leaving the group or facing a difficult situation. Create a generic hand stencil or have group members trace their own hands palm side down on poster paper and cut out the shape. Then, using the hand pattern, decorate the back of the *khamsa*. On the palm side of the *khamsa*, they create a good-luck message for the person to whom they are giving it.

Hopefully, after reading through this chapter, your creative juices are flowing and you are ready to design activities of your own, incorporating the various creative arts and accessing the different avenues through which students learn. Remember that the more variety you are able to offer teens when conducting activities, the more you will be tapping into their creative potentials.

REFERENCES

Bailey, S. 1997. Personal communication.

Gardner, H. 1985. *Frames of Mind: The Theory of Multiple Intelligences*. New York: Basic Books, Harper Collins Publishers.

Gomez, A. 1992. *Crafts of Many Cultures: 30 Authentic Craft Projects from Around the World*. New York: Scholastic Professional Books.

Finneran, L. 2000. *Drama Therapy with Special Populations*. Course Book, Kansas State University.

Nicholson-Nelson, K. 1998. *Develop Students' Multiple Intelligences*. New York: Scholastic Professional Books.

Oaklander, V. 1988. *Windows to Our Children*. New York: The Gestalt Journal Press.

Warren, B. 1993. *Using the Creative Arts in Therapy*. London: Routledge.

7

PACKING THE BAGS
FOR THE JOURNEY

Adolescent group facilitators recognize the need for preparedness and spontaneity for the journey. As contradictory as both those needs might be, they are essential for reaching the destination. The destination may be reached ahead of schedule or behind schedule. The timing of the arrival is of less importance than the journey itself. But if the guide is unaware of the destination, the fellow travelers will be even more clueless. Fellow travelers may occasionally take side trips to interesting sites, but they need to be reminded of the path and its eventual destination.

DRAMA THERAPY ACTIVITIES

Here are some drama therapy activities that you can place in your travel bag so you are ready to guide your young sojourners on some of the most amazing adventures of their lives. These activities are organized around specific topics of concern to adolescents. However, these activities may be interchanged since many of them may meet a variety of objectives. References to authors are noted. If no specific author is referenced, the activity has been adapted from a variety of sources.

Family Dynamics

Family Sculpting

Materials
Modeling clay

Purpose of the Activity

The purpose of this activity is to help youth to portray the family visually. It should be used when there is enough trust in the group to begin sharing more personal information. You could also use this to explore family dynamics in a piece of literature or in a family of historical significance.

Warm-up

Give teens some modeling clay and ask them to sculpt a family. Remind them to place family members in relationship to each other, closer or farther away, as they see the family relating to one another, and standing, sitting, or moving. Examine and talk about what each family member might be doing.

Directions

Have teens select a family they would like to learn more about. The person who formed the clay sculpture will serve as the sculptor, placing group members as they are placed in the clay sculpture. Encourage group members to use body posture, facial expression, gestures, and proximity to show their relationship to other members of the family. All persons should freeze into position after the sculptor has completed his work.

The facilitator then touches each member of the sculpture and asks that person to make one statement about his feelings. From this experience, the facilitator may start a scene, placing the persons in a situation of conflict. Or the facilitator may ask one person to respond to each frozen character. This activity can lead to many variations. After a scene, be sure to ask for different ways in which the scene might have been enacted.

Family Introduction

Materials

None

Purpose of the Activity

The purpose of this activity is to help group members become acquainted as they begin to expand their role repertoire.

Directions

Ask each individual to introduce herself to the group as someone else in the family might introduce her. Encourage each individual to assume the body posture, mannerisms, and vocal inflection of the designated family member.

Family Celebrations

Materials

None

Purpose of the Activity

This activity may be used to assess personal family dynamics or to examine family dynamics in a piece of literature or at a specific time and place in history.

Directions

Set up a family scene around a holiday or family celebration. Build the scene around a potential conflict that might arise at that time. You might want to start this scene with sculpting, as well. For example, before you begin the scene, you might set each member around the Thanksgiving table and encourage them to say what they are feeling and what they would rather be doing that day.

Peer Pressure

Party with a Purpose

(Nelson)

Materials

Slips of paper with designated roles listed:
Persuader: You will try to get someone to drink.
Mr. or Miss Sobriety: You are trying to remain sober.
Newcomer: You don't know anyone at the party.
Romeo (or Juliet): You are coming on to a new boyfriend or girlfriend.

Follower: You do whatever your friend suggests.

Designated Driver: You are responsible for getting your friends home safely.

I'll Never Do It Again: You have already drunk too much and thrown up. You swear you'll never drink again.

Out Like a Light: You have passed out, but probably nobody has noticed.

Curiosity: You haven't used pot, but you are curious about it.

Mediator: You try to get your friends to make peace with each other.

Arsonist: You are smoking and accidentally set the sofa afire.

Party Crasher: You haven't been invited, but you are sure everyone will be happy you've come.

Babysitter: You've brought your younger brother or sister to the party because you are responsible for him or her.

Younger Brother/Sister: You have come with your older brother or sister who is babysitting this evening. You have never drunk or used drugs.

Purpose of the Activity

The purpose of the activity is practice problem-solving skills in a safe environment. Encourage all group members to play the assigned role, whether or not it feels comfortable.

Directions

Each person draws a slip of paper with a role to play at the party. Persons must play their role effectively without showing others their assigned role, except for the younger/older brother/sister pairs. Facilitators may serve as hosts, who greet the party guests at the door. The facilitators can help to keep up the spontaneity and encourage all members to participate. Facilitators should let the action flow but feel free to call out "freeze" at any time they wish to change or stop the action.

Follow the scene with a discussion of the feelings connected with each role, the way in which each person reacted to the actions of others, and how they were or were not influenced by the behavior of others. Discuss what might have happened after the scene ended, as well as other ways the scene might have concluded.

Prom Stories

(Nelson)

Materials

Ball of yarn

Slips of paper with designated roles listed. You may use those listed below or create your own according to the issues you think need to be addressed by your group.

Glen (or Glenda): Your parents supplied the booze for your friends at the after-prom party this weekend. They think it is okay for you to drink as long as you drink at home.

Darla (or Doug): Your parents provided dinner and after-prom activities for you and your friends so that they would be safe and drug-free. At breakfast the next morning you and your friends are discussing the parties you missed the night before.

Gwen: You got drunk at an after-prom party this weekend. You don't exactly remember what happened. Your friends have informed you that you were exceptionally flirtatious and ended up in the bedroom with a couple of guys that you hardly know.

Bob (or Barbara): Your folks rented a room at a local hotel for your friends after the prom. Things got pretty rowdy, and the hotel is now charging your parents three hundred dollars for room damages. Your parents insist that you must pay for these damages.

Scott: After you left the prom, you got plastered and got in a really bad fight with two guys. You are eighteen years old and got picked up by the cops. You now face assault charges.

Vicky: Your date insisted that you have sex with him after the prom. He claimed you "owed it to him" since he had paid for the evening, including the dinner, dance, and flowers.

Jennifer: You attended the prom with two of your female friends because you did not have a date. You prepared dinner for your friends at your house and enjoyed the evening. But another of your friends is really mad at you because you danced with her date at the prom.

Jim: You couldn't afford to go to the prom, but you met a lot of your friends at a party afterwards. You met a really cute girl there, and she seemed to like you a lot. She claimed to be in "recovery" and refused to drink or smoke pot.

Marcy: You are a good student with high morals and have little use for kids who use drugs. You were pretty surprised when you showed up at a party after the prom and found that many of your friends were smoking pot, drinking, and making out in the bedroom.

Gene (or Jean): The week before the prom you worked hours and hours putting together an event you thought everyone would enjoy. Your date was pleasant, and you had a good time. But a group of friends insisted on criticizing the choice of music and decorations all evening. You are pretty upset with their behavior.

Randy: You have a long history of drinking, but during prom weekend you decided not to join in the festivities. You went on a camping trip instead. The fishing was great, but you are wondering what you missed out on by not attending the prom.

Susie (or Steve): You and your friends planned an alternative activity instead of attending the prom. You spent the day preparing a special meal and then enjoyed an evening of games and videos. Your peers think you are criticizing their activities.

Adam (or Angela): You drank a lot this weekend, but you hardly felt it. You notice that it takes more and more alcohol to provide you with the "buzz" you used to get after two or three drinks.

Purpose of the Activity

The purpose of the activity is to help teens see causal relationships and to engage in problem solving in a safe environment, where a variety of solutions may be explored.

Directions

Each person will draw a role for the prom. They must decide how to play the role and how to add details to the story they have been given. The first person starts telling his story, holding a ball of yarn. When the next person starts his story, the ball of yarn is handed to him, while the first person holds onto his end of the yarn. Continue in this manner until all the stories have been told. Note the tangled web created by all these stories. Group members then assist each person in becoming untangled by helping the person add to his story, starting with the last story and continuing backwards until the web is untangled. Debrief the stories and their significance once the activity is completed.

Following this exercise, discuss the stories that appeared most meaningful and how the pressure of peers influenced each character. Also discuss how the unraveling of the yarn web assisted each character.

Stereotypes

Materials

Sticky notes with assigned roles and responses listed on each. Add others you think would be appropriate.

Nerd—make fun of me
Jock—admire me
Clown—laugh with me
Prep—respect me
Druggie—doubt me
Punker—isolate me
Beautiful blonde—adore me
Class leader—listen carefully to me

Purpose of the Activity

The purpose of this activity is to examine stereotypes and how our reaction to others encourages those persons to respond in an expected manner. This activity is similar to the Labeling warm-up in Chapter 4, but it allows the group to examine stereotypes in more depth.

Directions

When teens enter the room, place a note on each person's forehead. You may use sticky notes or small pieces of paper attached

with masking tape. The notes will indicate the assigned role and
how others are to react to that individual. Set up a scene where all
these persons might be present, such as a class meeting. No one is
to tell the others what the assigned role happens to be, but all must
treat the individuals according to the instructions given. When the
action reaches a climax, freeze all persons. Have them guess what
their assigned role was. Then debrief with questions regarding how
it felt to have persons react to them in the same way, no matter
what they did. Ask each individual what she really wanted from
the group. Focus also on what the group would have had to do in
order to meet more of the needs of the individuals represented.

Future Projections

A Game Plan

(Nelson)

Materials

Small slips of paper
Pencils

Purpose of the Activity

The purpose of the activity is to encourage teens to set goals and
to enable them to see ways in which obstacles to their goals may
be overcome.

Directions

Each person writes down a personal goal for the year on a small
slip of paper. Collect these papers and shuffle them. Each person
draws another's goal. Set up the room like a football field, with
the goal post at one end. Each individual will start from one end
of the room and try to get to the goal. However, as he proceeds,
he must imagine the obstacles that might prevent him from
reaching his goal. Other group members portray those obstacles.
They must interact with the assigned player to see if he can overcome the obstacle and proceed. Audience members may cheer on
the player, as well as assist him in ways to overcome each obstacle. Conclude with a discussion of how it felt to meet each obstacle with the help of others.

My Dream

(adapted from Sternberg and Garcia 2000)

Materials

Small slips of paper
Pencils

Purpose of the Activity

The purpose of the activity is to expand role repertoire and to focus on the ability to reach one's goals.

Directions

Begin with a discussion of the term *dream* as a wish unfulfilled. Each person writes down a dream for herself on a small slip of paper. Collect papers and shuffle them. Each person draws the dream of another. Each participant will then enact the dream, establishing who she is, where she is, what is going on, and how she feels about living her dream. If participants get stuck, the facilitator may need to enter the scene to assist each person in adding more depth and meaning to the scene.

Conclude with a discussion of how it felt to enact someone else's dream, as well as how it felt to see your own dream enacted by another. Check to see how the dreams might have changed and which characters the group most identified with.

Fortune Telling

(adapted from Sternberg and Garcia 2000)

Materials

Crystal ball, cards, or tea leaves (or you may do this activity without any props)

Purpose of the Activity

The purpose of the activity is to engage youth in their imaginations and to focus on a future, no matter how unimaginable it might seem.

Directions

Divide the group into pairs. Each person will tell the future of his partner, imagining that he can see into a crystal ball, read his palm, or decipher the meaning of the tea leaves. Then switch roles so that the fortune teller is now having his own fortune told. Discuss how it felt to play each role, as well as the accuracy or inaccuracy of the fortunes.

Back to the Future

Materials

Toy telephone

Purpose of the Activity

The purpose of the activity is to see the relationship between the present and the future. It may serve as a nice termination exercise for persons nearing the end of their time with the group.

Directions

Ask each individual to imagine herself ten years into the future. Using a toy telephone, each individual will place a phone call to herself, saying what she is now doing, what she has learned in the last ten years, and what she wished she had done differently.

Spirituality

Medicine Wheel

(Nelson and Mahaffey)

Materials

Paper plates
Markers
Construction paper
Glue
Scissors
Glitter glue
Any other decorative items available

Purpose of the Activity

The purpose of the activity is for group members to see themselves as persons with both strengths and weaknesses. More mature youth may also begin to see the relationship between their strengths and their weaknesses.

Direction

Explain that the Native American medicine wheel represents the four areas of health: spiritual, emotional, intellectual, and physical. Give each person a paper plate and ask him to divide it into four areas. Each quadrant will represent one of the four areas of health. Provide participants items with which to decorate the plates. Once the art pieces are finished, explain that the each corner of the room will represent one of the areas of health. Ask each person to go to the area of the room that represents his strength. Request that each area prepare a movement that represents its strength. You might then ask each area of strength to move toward an area of weakness and incorporate the weakness into its strength or ask for all four areas to prepare a group movement together.

Conclude with a discussion of strengths and weaknesses and the ways in which strengths may be used to assist an area of weakness.

Gifts of the Human Spirit

(Nelson and Mahaffey)

Materials

Construction paper
Glue
Glitter glue
Colored tissue paper
Small scraps of wood
Acrylic paints
Any other available art materials
Newspaper
String, tape, or ribbon
Scissors

Purpose of the Activity

The purpose of this activity is to allow group members to experience the joy of both giving and receiving. It also focuses on those gifts that cannot be measured by wealth.

Warm-up

This exercise works best if it involves two separate sessions. Start with a warm-up that involves the passing around of an imaginary box. Each person must imagine that the box contains something that she really needs. Each person opens the box and pantomimes its contents by using the object. Briefly discuss gifts of the human spirit that might be needed by the group before proceeding to the next part of the exercise. Examples of these gifts might include self-esteem, respect, serenity, determination, or self-control. Provide a variety of art materials for participants and ask them to prepare an artistic object that represents such a gift of the spirit. Carefully explain that at the next session, this gift will be given to another group member.

Directions

Between sessions, wrap each gift in newspaper so it will not be recognized. At the next session, discuss the meaning of the term *guru* and what a guru does. One at a time, each person will choose a gift. The person who made the gift will assume the role of the guru, explaining to the receiver the significance of this human virtue and how it might be used. The person who receives the gift will give a response to the guru. Continue until all participants have received a gift.

Conclude with a discussion of how it felt to both give and receive such gifts and how the gifts might help each person.

Identity

The CD of Me

(Finneran)

Materials

CDs (perhaps old AOL or other Internet service provider CDs)

Plastic CD covers with blank front and back inserts
Peel-and-stick CD labels
Markers or other writing utensils
Scissors
Glitter glue (optional)
Old magazines for cutting collage pieces

Purpose of the Activity

The purpose of the activity is to help group members recognize their own strengths and celebrate their individuality.

Directions

Discuss the concept of a "musical journey." Ask youth to think about the life experiences they have had and how they might translate into music or songs. Give them time to prepare a CD label and a CD cover that best reflect their unique "musical journey." Some group members may actually want to write songs that would be on their personal CD.

Treasure Chests

(Nelson)

Materials

Shoe boxes
Paints
Scissors
Magazine pictures
Glue
Brushes
Any other available art materials

Purpose of the Activity

The purpose of the activity is to help teens recognize their own personal worth and to expand their role repertoire.

Directions

Introduce the concept of a treasure chest as a box of great personal value. Then provide the opportunity for group members to

Linda's treasure chest is filled with personal items that represent her.

prepare their own treasure chests, placing on the outside of the shoe box those images that represent the aspects of self they wish to make public to others. The inside of the box will be filled with personal objects, pictures, or other valuables that more personally represent themselves. Once the boxes are completed, ask each person to choose a box he finds intriguing and to pretend to be the owner of this treasure chest. He must then make up a story about this person, filling in the details of his life by examining the chest. At some point, discuss where the treasure chest might be hidden.

If nearing the end of a series of sessions, you might ask each person to place his own treasure chest at his feet. Ask all members to write a note of appreciation or admiration for every other person in the group and place the notes in the proper treasure chests.

My Tree House

(Finneran)

Materials

Tree branches
Square or rectangular pieces of wood with hole drilled in the
   center to hold the branch
Liquid nails
Glue
Glue gun
Glue sticks
Leaves
Plastic flowers
Popsicle sticks
Scrap wood
Throwaway objects made of wood, paper, or cardboard
Any other available art objects

Purpose of the Activity

The purpose of the activity is to allow teens to create a safe place
or hang out.

Directions

Ask the group to envision a giant, special tree where they
would like to build a dream tree house, known only to them
and any special persons they choose. Group members draw a
rough design of their tree house on a piece of paper, select a
tree branch, and create their dream tree house. Continue by
asking each person to tell a story about her tree house. You
may preface the activity by viewing clips from such movies as
Swiss Family Robinson or *The War*. You may also use this as a
warm-up to a more involved activity where teens create a
story about their tree house and enact that story for the rest of
the group.

Masks

Materials

Brown paper bags
Paper plates
Poster board
Plaster bandages (and petroleum jelly, hair band, shower cap, or bandana)
Paints
Brushes
Glue
Glitter glue
Colored tissue paper
Markers
Yarn
Scissors
Any other available art materials

Purpose of the Activity

The making of masks may serve a variety of purposes. Primarily they are used to assist group members in recognizing their own roles or potential roles.

Directions

Before preparing a mask, engage teens in a discussion of when and why masks are worn. Masks may be made out of a variety of materials, such as brown paper bags, paper plates, poster board, or plaster bandages. Masks may represent the public and private selves, the hero and the villain, or a favorite animal or character from a movie. If using plaster bandages, the group should be comfortable with each other and trusting enough to have other persons in their personal space. Cut plaster bandages in small strips about 1 1/2"–2" long. Each person must cover the face and eyebrows with petroleum jelly and use a hair band, shower cap, or bandana to keep the plaster out of his eyes. Be sure all makeup is removed before beginning this exercise. The group will be divided into pairs to complete the exercise. The plaster bandages will be wetted in water and placed gently on the face, leaving the

Lanell's mask is made of heavy felt soaked in white glue and dried over a face model then decorated.

eyes and nostrils open. Be careful that water does not drip into the eyes, ears, or mouth. Apply three or four layers of bandages, and allow the bandage to harden (about twenty minutes) before removing it from the face. Within twenty-four hours, the mask will harden enough to be painted on both sides.

Once the masks are painted, you may use them for a variety of activities. Teens may enact stories with the masks, write monologues for the masked character, or engage in dialogues with each other. A particularly effective technique involves the use of the partner. When the monologue is read, the partner stands and holds the mask in front of his face. The person who prepared the mask is hidden behind his partner as he reads his monologue.

Grief and Loss

Burden Bags

(Finneran)

Materials

   Brown paper lunch bags
   Beads
   Embroidery thread
   Glitter
   Sequins
   Feathers
   Small objects or totems
   Needles
   Glue
   Scissors
   3" x 5" note cards
   Pencils

Purpose of the Activity

The purpose of the activity is to identify the burdens carried and ways in which youth might lighten their loads.

Directions

Native American women actually designed and created the first backpacks. They developed a way to help carry heavy loads while gathering food, wood, and other items. Each bag was unique in that it was designed by the wearer and reflected her personal character (Carlson 1994). Relate this story of the "burden baskets" to youth. Discuss how the baskets made the loads carried by the women easier to manage. Instruct the group members to create their own personal "burden bags" that they will personally design with supplied materials or materials they bring in. They will then place inside the bag three note cards, each containing a current "burden" in their lives (increased family responsibilities, fighting parents, and so on). Using various creative arts activities, address each of the burdens and ways to lighten the load of each.

Sophia and the Heartmender

(Finneran)

Materials

Sophia and the Heartmender (Olofsdotter 1993)
Chalkboard, whiteboard, or large piece of paper
Scarves or fabrics

Purpose of the Activity

The purpose of the activity is to recognize both the things that break, as well as the things that heal, our hearts.

Directions

Read the story to the group. Display a large broken heart on a large piece of paper, whiteboard, or chalkboard. Brainstorm things that could break a person's heart. Facilitate a discussion about these items and see if you can find a common theme. Then ask the group to create a sculpture that represents that theme. You may use scarves and fabrics to help with the sculpture, if you desire. Then add a sound and word to the sculpture. Teens may even be encouraged to make a moving sculpture, if that seems more appropriate. Process the sculpture, noting how a person might deal with situations, people, and actions that might break a person's heart. Then brainstorm ways for a person to start the healing process, such as journaling or doing activities with friends or a support group. Teens may desire to create and enact scenes incorporating their ideas for healing. These enactments should be followed by an opportunity to evaluate the effectiveness of the suggestions.

Sculpting a Feeling

Materials
Modeling clay

Purpose of the Activity
The purpose of the activity is to visualize feelings.

Directions
Provide each group member with a ball of modeling clay. Ask participants to sculpt how they are feeling today. Then share the sculptures. Look for common themes and sculpt those feelings in small groups of three or four persons. Next add movement and sound to the feeling.

Fears

Monsters in Our Lives

(Finneran)

Materials
Markers
Crayons
Pencils
Paper plate

Purpose of the Activity
The purpose of the activity is to recognize how our fears drain our energies and to determine coping mechanisms to deal with those fears. This exercise can also explore literary and historical themes that deal with fear. *Note:* This activity may bring information to the surface from individuals in the group that would not be appropriate to share within the group (unless the group is a therapy group). Make sure that you establish safe boundaries for this activity. For example, when discussing people who may be monsters in our lives, instruct group members to keep that category generic in nature. You would not want to have a group member to name a specific person who abuses them in some way.

Directions

Brainstorm how a monster affects us. Lead the group into discussing monsters as things, people, and circumstances that drain our energy and pull strength from us as we go about our day-to-day activities. Using markers, crayons, pencils, and a paper plate, have participants create a mask that represents a particular "monster" in their lives at this moment. Then engage the group members in sharing their monsters and how they affect their lives. As a group, create a moving image of a "monster" that incorporates the main theme of each individual monster. Encourage the group to add words and phrases to the monster. Discuss ways that we can "tame" our monsters. Then enact the taming of the monster. Conclude by asking each person to make a sound that represents the drama experience. Then discuss how each person might best tame her monster.

Dragons

(Nelson)

Materials needed:

Air-drying clay
Acrylic paint
Brushes
Chalkboard, whiteboard, or flip chart
Markers

Purpose of the Activity

The purpose of the activity is to recognize how our fear protects us, as well as ways to overcome unnecessary fears. The exercise can also be tied in with literary and historical themes that deal with fear.

Directions

Brainstorm what the group knows about dragons. Discuss what a dragon looks like, where it lives, and what purpose it serves. Be certain you mention that the dragon appears so fearful because he is guarding some treasure of great worth. Provide teens with a ball of air-drying clay that may be used to create their dragon. After several hours, the dragons may be painted with acrylic paint. Several activities may then follow. The group might prepare a group cinquain. A cinquain is a five-line poem. The first line is simply the word "dragon." Line two should be two words that define or describe the dragon. Line three is three words that describe an action related to the dragon. Line four is four words that express an attitude toward or emotional feeling about the dragon. Line five is one word that sums up the previous four lines. The group could be encouraged to prepare a dragon sculpture, using each person as one part of the dragon (one for each leg, one for the head, and so on). Make the dragon come to life by moving across the room. Add sound to show how the dragon feels. Or the group could be encouraged to create a story about its dragon, enacting where the dragon might be found and how he might be overcome.

Conclude with a discussion of dragons in our own lives and the personal strengths we use to overcome our "dragons." This exercise could open up great discussion about how fear leads nations to war, politicians to corruption, and movie stars to poor lifestyle choices.

REFERENCES

Carlson, L. 1994. *More Than Moccasins*. Chicago: Chicago Review Press.

Mahaffey, J. 2001. Personal communication.

Olofsdotter, M. 1993. *Sofia and the Heartmender*. Minneapolis: Free Spirit Publishing.

Sternberg, P., and A. Garcia. 2000. *Sociodrama: Who's in Your Shoes?* Second Edition. Westport, CT: Praeger.

8

MILEAGE MARKERS

Maps are an essential part of almost any journey. Maps serve as a basic structure or guide and incorporate mileage markers, giving the traveler points from which to measure progress along the way. Some markers delineate fundamental tasks that must be accomplished in order for the journey to maintain forward progression. These functional markers become routines for daily living. Such routines are an important part of the adolescent's life. Adolescents engage in many routines throughout their day and find these routines comforting, providing them with familiar expectations. Rituals are more formal mileage markers on maps that acknowledge and celebrate specific moments along the journey. They provide anchor points to help ease transitions into the unfamiliar, allowing meaning to be made from both the ordinary and the obscure. Most adolescent rituals are highly symbolic, marking important events that give meaning to their lives. Mileage markers may vary from map to map, embodying the unique characteristics of the adolescent to whom the map belongs. It is important to consider first the role that routines play in the life of the adolescent, for from those routines or the lack thereof, adolescent rituals are created.

FUNCTIONAL MILEAGE MARKERS: ROUTINES

Physical Routines—Getting Started

Daily physical routines start with arising at a designated time and getting ready for school. Mornings and adolescents usually do not mix. The adolescent's internal clock is set to staying up late and sleeping in the next morning. Many adolescents find the dance

111

between themselves and their alarm clock an annoying one, but they usually resort to using an alarm to start their morning routine of preparing for a day at school. These morning routines are developmental in that certain aspects of the routines become more complex with age and become more the responsibility of the adolescent with less parental involvement. For example, a parent may select clothes for a young child to wear to school and even help the child with the physical aspects of getting dressed. The adolescent, on the other hand, is expected to select his clothes, dress himself, and complete his morning hygiene routine on his own.

With today's media focus on appearance, the morning hygiene routine can be very involved for adolescent females. Everything from showering to hair styling to applying makeup to selecting the perfect outfit must be contemplated. Of course, selecting the perfect outfit consists of many steps in and of itself. Different articles of clothing will be tried on, taken off, rejected as a possibility and tossed to the floor to join other items that weren't quite right. Many teen girls even phone their close friends to see what they may be wearing to school. Once the perfect outfit is put together, all of the trimmings including shoes, hair accessories, jewelry, and purses must be selected. This hygiene routine may well set the tone for the day's attitude. When the perfect outfit doesn't come together or it's a "bad hair" day, the adolescent female's attitude and confidence may be undermined. In addition, more and more adolescent males are also under pressure to live up to media scrutiny for their appearance and projected image. Many teen boys now spend considerable lengths of time prepping for the day ahead in much the same way as their female counterparts.

In the mind of many adolescents, breakfast is not an important meal, often skipped so more time can be spent on getting ready for the day. This typical morning routine takes a back seat to completing last-minute homework, meeting friends before classes begin, or sleeping as late as possible and then running to catch the bus. As adults, we know that breakfast is an important meal, providing the brain with much needed fuel for academic endeavors. In addition, adolescents who take prescription medications may need to take the meds with food. Thus, the breakfast battle is often a typical part of morning routines in homes across the country.

Physical Routines—Winding Down

Bedtime? What's that? Adolescents want to set their own time for turning out the lights. Usually, that is well past the time that their parents have called it a day. Their end-of-the-day routine may involve a variety of tasks, including completing homework assignments, gathering items for the next day's projects, calling or e-chatting with friends, journaling, pleasure reading, listening to music, playing music, and maybe catching some late-night television. For some, there are more hygiene routines to perform such as removing makeup, brushing teeth, skin cleansing, and taking prescribed medications. Oh, and that very important task—setting the alarm!

Social-academic Routines

Once at school, physical routines continue. However, they are now mixed with academic routines, such as getting to class on time, having the necessary materials, and participating in educational activities throughout the day, as well as social-emotional routines like meeting friends between classes, catching up on gossip, and planning for after school or weekend fun. Because the school day of an adolescent is packed with so many important routines, teachers and other adults must be prepared for a variety of interactions and reactions. How can studying about prepositions be important when one is thinking about getting a date to the school dance? Why is working hard in gym class important when one needs energy for that after-school job? Why is the teacher making such a big deal about having a pen rather than a pencil? What does all this have to do with *my* life anyway?

Because getting a good, solid education is important, teachers need to emphasize the use of routine in their classes. In a similar fashion, other helping professionals can benefit from these suggestions. Both social and academic routines need to be developed. Establishing a social routine for integrating and accepting students into a class sets the tone for listening, interacting, and learning. When students feel acknowledged and embraced, they are more likely to participate. Calling students by name when they enter, taking role, and engaging in social conversation are ways that adults can help students get comfortable and make that transition from the less structured hallway behavior to the learning environment.

Lesson Planning

Teachers learn about lesson planning as part of their college coursework for a reason. Good lesson plans incorporate academic maps for learning concepts. In this day and age of accountability, other organizations could benefit from similar planning and assessment procedures. Sometimes pre-tests are given to see what students know so that lessons do not become repetitious in nature. Having a course syllabus prepared is also helpful as it helps establish a linear progression of what will be introduced and when. Most lessons begin by introducing new vocabulary or concepts along with a preview of what the main lesson will involve. This beginning routine pulls the students into the lesson and gives them a solid knowledge base. During the lesson, students may complete study guides, keeping them active in the learning process. Following the main lesson, students often complete worksheets, quizzes, or write short papers over the topic studied. In addition, teachers often have students complete a project to demonstrate their knowledge of the topic. Portfolios are an excellent example of maintaining students' work, which can then be explored routinely with them throughout the course of the semester, allowing the student to track her progress. Some of the drama activities mentioned earlier in the book can also serve as a means of assessment, checking the acquisition of social skills, as well as the processing of historical, literary, or health information. Conducting lessons in this way, with a beginning, middle, and ending structure, is comforting to students and affords them the energy to anticipate new learning. They don't have to wonder what will happen next, which can create anxiety within them and interfere with their learning. Incorporating some of these procedures into your understanding of the group process can prove quite beneficial.

However, a word of caution must be issued here. Too much

routine in any structure can be boring. Bored adolescents soon zone out! Mixing routine with some intrigue and novelty is important as long as it is done in a manner that is emotionally safe for all students. And, speaking of emotional safety, adults also need to set a routine for how feedback is given to students. The routine might be to speak individually to students when discussing information of a personal nature and communally when discussing information pertinent to the overall lesson, deadlines, or group structure.

Discipline

Additionally, facilitators need a routine for discipline. What is the hierarchy for disciplinary issues? Are students sent to an authority immediately, or is there a process set up to solve behavior problems in the group or class? Teens may complain about a disciplinary structure but are actually relieved to have one in place, since not knowing what to expect or having to guess what to expect equals stress. A routine for discipline makes the classroom or group a safe, established place in which to be and learn. Disciplinary issues can become negative routines for adolescents. Being tardy, using foul language, refusing to participate, distracting others, and not following directions are just a few negative routines that students can quickly develop. Since routines are habitual in nature, the sooner negative routines are addressed, the better. Holding adolescents accountable will actually make them feel more appreciated and acknowledged. There may be intense moments initially when establishing acceptable and appropriate disciplinary routines and keeping them consistent, but once teens realize these routines are for their overall safety, they will usually accept them. For those who don't, that routine of managing feedback comes into play. It is best to handle these situations individually and away from the whole class.

What adolescents experience in school or in a prevention setting carries over to the outside world. Positive routines and skills learned there become positive skills and routines at work or at home. Teens who realize the importance of being on time to class or group also realize the importance of being on time to their after-school job. Students who realize that what they are learning is important to their future will more likely place importance on completing homework. If negative routines like those mentioned earlier are allowed at school, what more dangerous and risky negative routines will be engaged in outside of school? Smoking, drinking, and sex are outside negative routines in which adolescents may become involved.

Bridging to After-school Routines

Furthermore, teachers can impact how routines outside of the school day can be built to make transitions easier. This is especially true for special education teachers and those who work with them. The teachers often work with students, parents, and other adults on a student's IEP (Individual Education Plan) team to establish safe and appropriate activities for the student. These activities may include a supported work experience, community social activities with youth specialist or attendant care worker support, and supervised daily living activities. In supported work experiences, a job coach accompanies students to model on-the-job skills and behaviors, provide encouragement and feedback, and slowly consign job tasks to the student until he is able to manage the job without the support. Special education students often need this routine when starting out on a job. They aren't bombarded by too much at once and the chances of being happy and successful on the job are greater. Youth specialists and attendant care workers are usually employees of local agencies paid to accompany students to activities in the community. Their role is similar to that of the job coach. Some school districts also provide support for students who need to learn daily living skills such as laundry, cooking, or grocery and hygiene shopping.

Social-emotional Routines

Adolescents are social-emotional beings. Their peers are the most important and influential individuals in their lives, their lifeline to emotional well-being. Their social-emotional routines are the most prominent aspects of their lives and a motivator to attend school and other groups. They must have their daily dose of peer interactions in order to feel complete. Social routines at school may include meeting friends at a designated place before school starts, between class check-ins, congregating in the school cafeteria, and that after-school "What are you doing tonight?"

planning. There are after-school sports events, clubs, and other activities that are social congregating points for teens. Once home, there is the overwhelming need to call, email, or hang with friends. It is often difficult for parents to understand why their teen son or daughter has to be surrounded in some manner by their cohorts every evening.

For every social routine, there is an emotional counterpart, often influenced by hormones. We can all identify with the highs and lows of wins and losses in sports, whether participant or observer. Remember the feelings attached to being picked first for an activity? Being picked last? Or not being picked at all? Many dramas are played out each day at home, at school, at a job, and elsewhere that affect the social-emotional side of the adolescent's life. Whether positive or negative, the emotional roller coasters that adolescents encounter throughout their day such as breakups, dating snafus, unexpected sightings of a love interest, grades, and other assorted happenings may lead to emotional overload. Without daily routines to lend them some benign structure, adolescents might completely fall apart.

FORMAL MILEAGE MARKERS: RITUALS

Routines become rituals when mere tasks become symbolic acts. As with routines, there are many types of, styles of, and layers to rituals. Rituals provide adolescents with ways to acknowledge and celebrate milestones in their development, heal from letdowns or loss, connect with significant others, or explore meaning in life. Rituals give meaning to shared joys, woes, changes, and risks. Through rituals, adolescents are able to observe their emotional connections to others, providing them with a sense of identity and purpose. Whether planned or spontaneous, rituals are a central part of the journey. When physical, social-emotional, academic, or spiritual changes occur and are consciously acknowledged, they become ceremonial rites of passage for the adolescent. They may be public, private, or secret and symbolized in a variety of ways. Like routines, they may be positive or negative in nature. In fact, rituals do not always involve words, special occasions, ceremonial leaders, or an audience. Therefore, some of the most powerful rituals are ones that are self-reflective in nature.

Physical Rituals

Adolescence brings many physical rites of passage. Probably the most important physical marker of adolescence is menarche for females and first ejaculation for males. In many cultures, these physical events determine admission into adulthood. Other physical rites of passage may include developing breasts and body hair, getting a body piercing or tattoo, that first kiss from that first love, or the first sexual encounter. Once persons turn thirteen, they are officially teenagers. Traditional rituals acknowledging this mileage marker include the Bas Mitzvah or Bar Mitzvah. From there, the physical milestones for birth dates are turning eighteen and twenty-one. Each of those ages brings with it added responsibilities and new opportunities previously unavailable to the adolescent.

Academic Rituals

Even though the first official day of school happened earlier on the map at a point called kindergarten, the first day of junior high or middle school is a definite rite of passage. Now the adolescent will encounter several teachers throughout his school day. He will be required to maneuver himself through a maze of hallways, master the locker combination, and be given added academic responsibilities. Soon comes high school. Even though it is similar to junior high, there is something about high school that gives an added layer of independence to and pressure on the adolescent. New rituals will be incorporated into the school day. Teachers may require a ritualistic period of silent reading during the week to honor the importance of reading in life, whether for school or for pleasure. There may be awards ceremonies for sports, academics, and extracurricular activities. Each academic ceremony contains specific rituals students must follow. For example, at graduation ceremonies, students enter in alphabetical order, receive their diploma with their left hand and shake hands with the right, move their tassels in a certain direction following the announcement that they are officially graduated, and then celebrate by throwing their hats in the air and whooping it up. Spring break is a ritual with many schools across the country. For seniors, it is usually the first time they head off with friends for a vacation rather than with their families. As mentioned earlier in this chapter, there are positive and negative rituals. During spring break, students often engage in negative rituals such as drinking or having sex.

Social-emotional Rituals

Social-emotional rituals are among the most meaningful types of rituals for the adolescent. School dances, first dates, that first car, first job, and initiations are some of the most important. Learning rituals of the social pecking order is also vital. Almost every school has its own traditions and rituals that students are encouraged to follow. For example, seniors may have the right to select where to sit in the cafeteria while sophomores and juniors are required to sit with their teachers. Underclassmen may have to perform certain tasks for upperclassmen during spirit week. School dances, like homecoming and prom, are loaded with rituals: selecting the right dress, purchasing the corsage or boutonniere, choosing the restaurant, and posing for a picture at the dance. Prior to the dance there is the ritual preparation of the dance space. Following the dance there are often parties to attend.

Initiation rituals of adolescence may include acceptance into a club, sports team, academic society, or even a gang. Gang initiations may involve many rituals, some very risky. There are specific rituals for being *jumped in* or *jumped out* of a gang. These rituals are usually physical in nature, and often require beatings, piercing, tattoos, or sexual activities. In addition, many academic sororities and fraternities also engage in risky initiations in which newcomers are hazed. Adolescents heading off to college may be faced with such initiations when pledging a sorority or fraternity.

Spiritual Rituals

Spiritual rituals are not necessarily religious based. These rituals may involve meditation, contemplation, or introspection. Meditation has long been a way for people to relax and focus. Through meditation rituals, adolescents may be able to accomplish the task of relaxation and self-direction, avoiding the need for medication to achieve the same end. Therapists have had success using meditative work and biofeedback with adolescents who are anxious or fearful about school or social situations. Some high schools now offer yoga and tai chi as part of their curriculum. Again, some of the most powerful rituals are those involving self-reflection.

In conclusion, adults need to recognize the important role that routines and rituals play in the lives of adolescents. Having a solid structure or base from which to branch out makes the journey through adolescence safer, more pleasurable, and less chaotic. Since routines form this base, it is critical for adults to establish them early on in a child's life so that when the young child ventures into the world of adolescence, with all its intensities, complexities, and increasing responsibilities, she will be better prepared to follow the map and move smoothly along the journey toward adulthood. Creating and establishing rituals to mark specific spots on the map are essential to forming the adolescent's life footprint. Development of such a life footprint allows the adolescent to connect with her past, define her present, and plan for her future.

In our disjointed, contemporary society some of the more traditional rituals for youth have either disappeared or lost some of their meaning. Oftentimes, youth live at quite a distance from their extended family so that even the important rituals such as graduation, prom, and confirmation are not shared with those family members, unlike past generations. Helping professionals are often invited to participate in those traditional events. More importantly, however, those professionals may assist adolescents in preparing safe, meaningful rituals of their own to mark significant events, developing their unique and personal mileage markers.

Transitions

Periods of transition are especially important times for ritual and adolescence is full of important transitional periods.

> Rituals are also about transitions from one social state to another so they guide us through changes in a specific way. Rituals of birth and death, coming of age and so on, enable us to let go of our current role and status and be affirmed in the new role and status. (Jennings 1998, 103)

Beginning Transitions

Following are some examples developed by the authors to assist adolescents in creating meaningful rituals, celebrations, and rites of passage. Let us begin with the transition that occurs at the beginning of an experience. In earlier chapters we shared with you many warm-up activities that can help youth feel more comfortable with one another. However, as adolescents start a new experience, they may need to mark that beginning in a more significant manner. For example, Linda Nelson served as the coordinator for the International Baccalaureate (IB) Diploma Program at her high school for three years. When the first IB class entered that high school, she prepared a formal initiation ceremony for all persons who were entering the program. She asked parents to bring a walking stick to present to their child. As a part of the drama of the initiation, parents came forward with their teen, handing over the walking stick to assist them on their journey toward their IB Diploma. At the conclusion of the formal initiation and pinning ceremony, all members of the IB class decorated those walking sticks with feathers, beads, and ribbons to symbolize the school, their connection with one another, and other special features. Everything from hockey sticks to limbs off trees planted the year of the child's birth were presented to those young people.

As this IB Diploma Program developed, other beginning rituals were established. Each year as sophomores entered the building, they were invited to a breakfast or picnic just prior to the beginning of the school year. Of course, they engaged in some warm-up activities described earlier in this book. But, they also participated in preparing a piece of art that contained within it something unique about each individual. For example, one year they were given puzzle pieces to decorate. Then they had to assemble the puzzle. Later on it was finished and framed as a symbol of that graduating class. Another year the sophomores were given air-drying clay and rocks to prepare a structure that represented something important to them. They were later strung as a mobile. Each of these classes also had a scrapbook person who assembled pictures and other remembrances of the class that served as a reminder of their time together. And, of course, there were the inevitable T-shirts. Those visible statements of who we are and where we have been continue to appeal to teens. When and where they wear them serve as important reminders of their significance.

Ending Transitions

The other significant time of transition occurs at the end of an experience. Lanell teaches in a therapeutic classroom located in a mental health center. Her classroom is open to local school students dealing with depression, anxiety, or other internalizing mental health issues. When students in her classroom were moved from their familiar setting into a new building, staff and students engaged in a good-bye ritual. Since this setting was being razed, writing on the walls of the empty classroom was permissible. Staff and students were instructed to take markers and write or draw on the walls representations of what they wanted to leave behind and what they wanted to take with them to the new building. Some students wrote thank-you notes to the space; others drew pictures of what the space meant to them, both positive and negative. As a part of the good-bye ritual, staff and students walked around the room to observe each other's work. They then verbally processed the experience. During this processing, some students actually placed themselves in various parts of the room and shared memories.

Ceremonial Transitions

Other ceremonial activities can also recognize the significance of personal accomplishments. For example, Lanell takes her adolescent students on a transitional journey at the end of each academic year to honor academic achievements, recognize individual accomplishments, and celebrate movement from one grade to another. Students, their families, classroom staff, and helping professionals who have worked with them throughout the year meet at Clinton Lake for the annual FriDay at the Lake. The day begins with an informal breakfast and quickly moves into students and adults engaging in a variety of games and conversations. Some play board games. Some play card games. Some choose more physical activities such as bocce ball, croquet, or the infamous drive-the-axe-deepest-into-the-hedge tree stump chal-

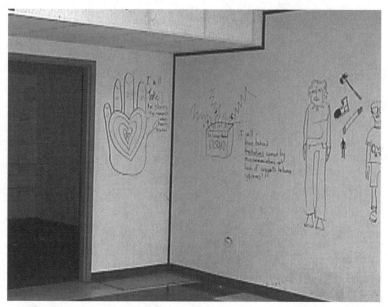

Lanell's corner of the good-bye wall, a closing ritual she engaged in with her students.

lenge. Of course, all look forward to the opportunity to compile their own bucket of water balloons to throw at each other. The picnic shelters are the safe zones but all other areas are open for warfare. Since the rules of the classroom also apply at the lake, students respect those who don't like to get wet by not attacking them. At noon, everyone assists in cooking burgers or hot dogs and feasting on the wide array of veggies, fruits, deviled eggs, and chips. For dessert, there is cake or cheesecake chosen by the students or staff who have summer birthdays. Of course, we first light candles and sing to each the traditional birthday song. Next comes the revered rite of passage ceremony witnessed by all in attendance. Sitting in a prominent area, Lanell calls each student forth, one by one, and reviews with them their achievements and accomplishments over the past year and collaboratively sets a goal for the year to come. Each student then opens a package filled with goodies reminiscent of the past year, marking special moments pertinent to him. The student is given an opportunity to be self-reflective and make any statements to the group about his personal experiences, achievements, challenges, and hopes for the future. It is also a time to recognize the important role others have played in his life. This ceremony is usually accompanied by laughter, tears, and connected moments of silence. To conclude the event, students are given the chance to take part in a water balloon launching challenge. For the water balloon challenge, students fill balloons, select a marker and write on the balloons negative aspects of the past year they would like to leave behind or let go of, and launch those balloons into oblivion. Often, parents are the ones holding the launcher, thus assisting their adolescent son or daughter in this purging process. By late afternoon, everyone helps clean the site, pack up, and head home for the weekend. This ceremonial ritual to end the school year is eagerly anticipated by all and is quickly the topic of conversation as new students enter the classroom.

Each group demands its own unique and creative expressions. The authors have sprinkled stardust on graduating seniors as a parting ritual, written endless personal messages to youth at the culmination of an experience, handed out polished stones as representations of remembrance, and taken countless pictures. Remember that drama engages all the senses, and as you are moving, singing, writing, or making art, you are engaged in drama. Those of us who work with adolescents are privileged to be a part of these very significant experiences and assisting them in creating their own mileage markers.

REFERENCES

Biziou, B. 2000. *The Joy of Family Rituals: Recipes for Everyday Living.* New York: St. Martin's Press.

Imber-Black, E., J. Roberts, and R. Whiting, eds. 1988. *Rituals in Families and Family Therapy.* New York: W. W. Norton & Company.

Jennings, S. 1998. *Introduction to Dramatherapy.* Philadelphia: Jessica Kingsley.

9

ROADSIDE ASSISTANCE

If you have become inspired along this journey, you may wish to become more involved with a variety of creative arts therapy associations. Each of them sponsors an annual conference and provides valuable resources for your use. Conferences are a great way to get acquainted with the latest developments in the field. They also provide excellent avenues for professional networking. These associations welcome membership from interested persons and professional organizations for those who meet criteria for professional registration.

Whether or not you decide to work on professional registration through one of these organizations, you will find their resources to be exceptionally helpful along your journey. When you get stuck or feel isolated because no one else in your organization or community understands what you are doing, check into one of these groups for that roadside assistance.

CREATIVE ARTS THERAPIES ASSOCIATIONS

Each of the creative arts (drama, music, art, poetry, and dance/movement) has its own national association that provides guidance and support to its members, establishes guidelines and regulations for its profession, and creates a networking opportunity for creative arts therapists and allied professionals to communicate.

Drama Therapy:
National Association for Drama Therapy (NADT)

The National Association for Drama Therapy defines drama therapy as "the systematic and intentional use of drama/theatre

125

processes, products, and associations to achieve the therapeutic goals of symptom relief, emotional and physical integration and personal growth" (www.nadt.org). For further information, contact The National Association for Drama Therapy, 15 Post Side Lane, Pittsford, NY 14534. Phone: 585-381-5618, Fax: 585-383-1474, e-mail: office@nadt.org or visit the Web site: www.nadt.org.

Poetry Therapy:
National Association for Poetry Therapy (NAPT)

Poetry therapy is a form of bibliotherapy and is "unique in its use of metaphor, imagery, rhythm, and other poetic devices. Poetry therapy involves the intentional use of poetry and other forms of literature for healing and personal growth" (www.poetrytherapy.org). For further information, contact The National Association for Poetry Therapy, 525 SW 5th Street, Suite A, Des Moines, IA 50309-4501. Phone: 1-866-844-NAPT, Fax: 515-282-9117; e-mail: info@poetrytherapy.org or visit the Web site: www.poetrytherapy.org.

Art Therapy:
The American Art Therapy Association (AATA)

Art therapy is defined as "a human service profession that uses art media, images, the creative process, and patient/client responses to the created products as reflection of an individual's development, abilities, personality, interests, concerns, and conflicts" (www.arttherapy.org). For more information, contact The American Art Therapy Association, 1202 Allanson Road, Mundlein, IL 60060-3808. Phone: 888-290-0878 or 847-949-6064, Fax: 847-566-4580, e-mail: info@arttherapy.org or visit the Web site: www.arttherapy.org.

Music Therapy:
American Music Therapy Association (AMTA)

Music has been used since the beginning of time to communicate and express feelings. "Music therapy unites the fields of music and therapy to provide a creative treatment and medium. More specifically, music therapy combines music modalities with humanistic, psychodynamic, behavioral, and biomedical approaches to help clients attain mental, physical, emotional, and/or spiritual goals. Problems or needs are addressed both through the therapeutic relationship between the client and music therapist, as well as approached directly through the music itself" (www.musictherapy.org). For further information, contact The American Music Therapy Association, 8455 Colesville Rd, Suite 1000, Silver Spring, MD 20910. Phone: 301-589-3300, Fax: 301-589-5175, e-mail: info@musictherapy.org or visit the Web site: www.musictherapy.org.

Psychodrama: American Society of Group Psychotherapy and Psychodrama (ASGPPA)

Psychodrama is a therapeutic discipline that uses "action methods, sociometry, role-training, and group dynamics to facilitate constructive change in the lives of participants. By closely approximating life situations in a structured environment, the participant is able to re-create and enact scenes in a way that allows both insight and an opportunity to practice new life skills" (www.asgpp.org). For further information, contact The American Society of Group Psychotherapy and Psychodrama, 301 N. Harrison Street, Suite 508, Princeton, NJ 08540. Phone: 609-452-1339, Fax: 609-936-1659, e-mail: asgpp@asgpp.org or visit the Web site: www.asgpp.org.

Dance/Movement Therapy:
The American Dance Therapy Association (ADTA)

Dance involves the direct expression through the body, making it an intimate and powerful medium for therapy. Based on the assumption that body and mind are interrelated, dance/movement therapy is defined by the American Dance Therapy Association as "the psychotherapeutic use of movement as a process which furthers the emotional, cognitive and physical integration of the individual. Dance/movement therapy effects changes in feelings, cognition, physical functioning, and behavior" (www.adta.org). For more information, contact: The American Dance Therapy Association, 2000 Century Plaza, Suite 108, 10632 Little Patuxent Parkway, Columbia, MD 21044. Phone: 410-997-4040, Fax: 410-997-4048, e-mail: info@adta.org or visit the Web site: www.adta.org.

Specifics regarding education, training, supervision, and other aspects of creative arts therapies can be obtained by visiting the Web sites of each creative arts therapy association or by writing their national offices. In addition, NCCATA (National Coalition of Creative Arts Therapies) has a Web site which also discusses each of the aforementioned creative arts therapies associations. The Web site for NCCATA is www.ncata.com. The International Expressive Arts Therapy Association (IEATA) is another arts therapy group. The Web site and contact information for IEATA is International Expressive Arts Therapy Association (IEATA), P.O. Box 320399, San Francisco, CA 94132-0399. Phone: 415-522-8959, e-mail: ieata@ieata.org or visit the Web site: www.ieata.org.

Educational Theatre Connections

There are two major educational theatre associations in the United States, American Alliance for Theatre in Education and the Education Theatre Association. On an international level, there is the International Drama/Theater and Education Association. Contact information for these associations is American Alliance for Theatre in Education (AATE), 7475 Wisconsin Avenue, Suite 300A, Bethesda, MD 20814. Phone: 301-951-7977, e-mail: info@aate.com or visit the Web site: www.aate.com. Education Theater Association, 2343 Auburn Avenue, Cincinnati, OH 45219. Phone: 513-421-3900 , Fax: 513-421-7077, or visit the Web site: www.edta.org. International Drama/Theater and Education Association (IDEA), P.O. Box 866, Brisbane, Albert ST BC Queensland, Australia 4002. Phone: 617-3359-2238 or 617-3309-1936, e-mail: idea@drama australia.org.au, or visit the Web site: http://educ.queensu.ca/~idea.

NETWORKING: IT'S YOUR LIFELINE

Many helping professionals who use the creative arts feel isolated in their work and eventually burn out trying to cover all the requirements of their respective jobs, explain the definition of their specific approach to allied professionals and/or others, and prove the value of their approach. For these reasons alone, creative arts therapists need a way to network. Communication among them is vital to their performance on the job, their professional development, and their own sense of creativity and accomplishment.

Each creative arts therapy association has a Web site listing regional contacts. You may wish to access these organizations as you continue to explore your use of drama with adolescents. Creative arts therapists regularly access this information to connect with others in their geographical area, whether they practice drama, poetry, art, music, psychodrama, or dance/movement therapy.

Establishing a creative arts therapy network at a job site or within a community or local region can help prevent burn out. Spending time with other creative arts persons, whether by phone, e-mail, or in person, can lessen the burden of isolation, lend credence to one's work, and spark new ideas, even if one isn't a creative arts therapist but uses the creative arts in his or her work.

Many creative arts therapists are also certified in other professional fields such as social work, special education, and counseling. It is wise to connect with the organizations associated with each of the areas in which one is certified to maintain up-to-date information about research, current work in the field, and connect with others who do similar work. A few of such professional organizations are Council for Exceptional Children (CEC) www.cec.sped.org, American Counseling Association (ACA) www.counseling.org, National Dissemination Center for Children with Disabilities (NICHCY) www.nichcy.org, and National Association of Social Workers (NASW) www.naswdc.org.

IS YOUR PROFESSIONAL BATTERY DEAD?

Recharge It: Tips for Professionals

What happens as the "professional battery" begins to lose juice? How does one keep that passion for the job going? Following are ten suggestions for recharging the battery and regaining one's enthusiasm for conducting intense work with adolescents. As you read through the list you will probably come up with some suggestions of your own.

1. Take a day off. Yes, that's right. Helping professionals need a personal day occasionally just to relax and replenish the creative juices within. Spend that day in whatever way allows you to find the healthy balance between self and work.

2. Attend a workshop, seminar, or conference. Spend time with other helping professionals discussing, practicing, and learning new techniques and ideas. Even consider presenting at some point in your career to share your knowledge and experience. You will be surprised how validating that can be.

3. Buy or check out a new book. Find a book that interests you professionally. Perhaps it is in an area related to your current area of expertise or perhaps it is an area about which you would like to learn more. Money spent on building one's professional library is money well spent.

4. Take a trip. Make time to observe someone else's work. Often, observing others sparks ideas within that can lead to new approaches and techniques.

5. Take up a new hobby or revive an old one. Hobbies are therapeutic. They are ways in which individuals find pleasure and accomplishment.

6. Treat yourself to therapy. All helping professionals will, at some point in their careers, need an opportunity to engage in personal therapy. The work you do is, by nature, very stressful. Using personal therapy as a professional avenue to dispose of that stress can be revitalizing. This may be a traditional type of therapy, a creative arts therapy, a massage, or another type of therapy suitable to you.

7. Join a professional organization. Being part of a professional organization lends credence to the work you do. It also connects you with others in the same or similar professions that can help create that professional network as well as enhance and strengthen your sense of professional identity.

8. Take a class. It is never too late to learn new things. Education is a lifelong process. Perhaps the class has no direct connection to your professional career. Community parks and recreation departments often sponsor classes in painting, photography, needlework, aerobics, dance, computers, or some other interest area.

9. Read, write, and publish. Take that knowledge and experience dancing around in your head and put it on paper so that others can benefit from what you have learned and developed. It can be as short as an article for a local newspaper or as long as an entire book.

10. Volunteer. What? That is supposed to recharge my battery? Well, yes, it does. As often as you like, volunteer somewhere in your local community. Volunteers are constantly in need. Tasks range from simply doing filing for a nonprofit agency, taking an elderly person to an appointment, to leading a group activity at a local shelter. Volunteering can rekindle one's sense of belonging and enhance one's meaning of life.

Our journey together has now come to a close. Hopefully this journey has given you ideas for adding more creativity, energy, and excitement to the groups you facilitate with youth. As each journey brings us in contact with new persons, places, and events, we become a part of those experiences, and the experiences become a part of us. May you continue your successful work with the adolescents in your care, and may they share their journey with you in a manner that is both productive and delightful for all of you.